Discovery Guide to

Cairo

including the Pyramids and Saqqara

by Michael Haag

Other *Discovery Guides* cover Egypt, Zimbabwe, West Africa, Jordan and the Holy Land, Aegean and Mediterranean Turkey, Eastern Turkey, Rajasthan, Vietnam, etc.

For our complete list, please write to:
Michael Haag Limited
PO Box 369
London NW3 4DP
England

Discovery Guide to Cairo, third edition
Text and photographs © 1990 by Michael Haag

Cover photographs by Michael Haag; cover design by Colin Elgie

Typeset in 9/10pt Compugraphic Palacio by BP Integraphics, Bath, Avon
Printed by litho in Great Britain by the Bath Press, Lower Bristol Road, Bath
BA2 3BL

Published by Michael Haag Limited, PO Box 369, London NW3 4DP, England

ISBN 0 902743 73 2

CONTENTS

*Practical Information sections follow most chapters, and there is
an appendix and an index at the rear.*

DISCOVERY GUIDES

'What one can imagine always surpasses what one sees, because of the scope of the imagination, except Cairo, because it surpasses anything one can imagine.'
—The qadi of Fez, quoted by Ibn Khaldun

'. . . and how should Cairo be otherwise when she is the Mother of the World?'
— 'Tale of the Jewish Doctor', *The Book of a Thousand Nights and a Night*, translated by Sir Richard Burton

No other city, with the possible exception of Rome, presents such a treasure of important and beautiful monuments, many of them still as they were in the Middle Ages. Add to this the line of Old Kingdom pyramids that runs along the rim of the Western Desert within sight of Cairo and you have within your compass a storehouse of human achievement that surpasses anything in the world.

Rome is part of our heritage and we are all more or less familiar with its story. Its streets and monuments have an immediate meaning. But the very antiquity of Egypt's past can elude comprehension, and for the West the culture of Islam has been the subject of studied ignorance. Too many people come to Cairo unaware, and leave it unexplored. Here a guide cannot help if it only describes, and lists statistics of age and size, but fails to explain the significance of what is seen.

And so this Discovery Guide tells the story of Cairo, of Giza, Memphis and Saqqara, and weaves this narrative into its itineraries. The desert pyramids themselves tell why they were built and how they in turn helped build a civilisation; and the mosques along the narrow medieval streets of the city recall the struggles and glories of Islam. This is an introduction to a strange but absorbing world, marking its salient moments and features, making it familiar—and perhaps encouraging you towards greater intimacies.

At the end of most chapters are *Practical Information* sections; that following the first chapter is comprehensive in its details on accommodation, eating places, shopping, travel, etc. And at the back of the guide is a chronology, a glossary and an explanation of Arabic numerals.

All information was up to date when going to press, but inflation and changing circumstances can have their effect. The reader is asked, therefore, to help keep this guide up to date by sending us any information that will help with the next edition. Please write to the *General Editor, Discovery Guide to Cairo, Michael Haag Limited, PO Box 369, London NW3 4DP, England.* Thank you.

CAIRO: MOTHER OF THE WORLD

From the air Cairo is a city of circles and radiating avenues at the head of the Nile Delta, its houses and buildings dull brown as though camouflaged to blend with the impinging desert. The colour is of the local stone, but also the residue of sandstorms which sometimes dust the city. At sundown you can see a thin layer of sand clinging to the polished dome of the Mohammed Ali Mosque atop the Citadel, and as you walk along the cracked pavements the desert wells up from below.

Like a great lung the Nile breathes through the city, but away from the broad slow-flowing river Westernised Cairo can have a heavy, airless feeling, an architectural jumble of fake pharaonic, blocklike modern, unnoticed art-deco and oppressive Victorian. Yet further east against the Moqat-tam Hills minarets like blades of tall grass rise against the sky, marking the old Islamic city of hidden beauty and palpitating energy which lends all Cairo its excitement.

In spirit Cairo remains as it began, an Arab encampment on the edge of the desert: hot, dry, the smell of dung, glowing coals and musk, lively with throngs of people. To this sprawling caravanserai come visitors from all over the Arab, African and Asian world, fantastically varied in colour, dress, characteristics, yet easily talking, mingling, bargaining like distant villagers meeting again in their market town.

For Cairo is the largest city in Africa and the political and cultural fulcrum of the Arab world. Its population has been officially estimated at eight million, and that itself represents a doubling over the past two decades, but as many as 14 million people could be living here. It has always attracted people from the villages of the valley and the Delta, but owes its recent staggering growth to the damage inflicted on the Suez Canal towns during the wars with Israel. At rush hours the buses threaten to burst or collapse with the pressure of Cairenes scrambling through doors and windows or clinging on outside for the long ride to or from the suburbs of Heliopolis, Maadi and Helwan.

But as the sun sets over the Nile the present slips away into timelessness, and from a high window over the river you can see the Pyramids at Giza glow gold against the Western Desert as they have done for one million, seven hundred thousand evenings past.

History of the City

Your orientation about the city is aided by a knowledge of its history, and its history, as with so much else in Egypt, is linked to the Nile.

5

In the Old Kingdom the capital of Egypt was at **Memphis**, 20 km to the south of present-day Cairo—but at that time the Delta had not pushed as far north as it has today and Memphis stood closer then to the conjunction of the Delta and the valley, controlling Egypt to the north and south. In this strategic sense Cairo is heir to Memphis, for the Nile divides just to the north of the capital.

Ancient **Heliopolis**, its scant ruins near a modern suburb bearing the same name at the northeast of the city enroute to the airport, was once the religious centre of Egypt, and in pharaonic times there was a settlement, perhaps even a town, on the east bank of the Nile opposite the island of Roda, but Cairo cannot be said to have developed out of these, and even its connection with what is now called Old Cairo is tenuous. In Roman and Byzantine times when there was a fortress here, Old Cairo was called **Babylon in Egypt**, probably a Greek corruption of the ancient name of Roda, *Per-Hapi-en-Yun,* House of the Nile of Heliopolis. Fortress rather than administrative centre was sufficient role for the settlement, and Babylon never amounted to much. In the last centuries before Christ, Egypt was ruled by Alexander's successors, the Ptolemies, from their Mediterranean capital, Alexandria.

The Arab conquest

It was the Arabs, for whom the desert and not the sea provided familiar lines of communication, who developed the logic of the site. In AD 641, Amr arrived in Egypt at the head of a small army and both Alexandria and Babylon opened their gates to him. Amr was enchanted with Alexandria and wrote back to the Caliph at Medina that this should be the Muslim capital of the conquered country, but Omar replied, 'Will there be water between me and the Muslim army?' Amr returned to Babylon where only sand separated him from Arabia; the tent (*fustat*) he had pitched there before marching on Alexandria was still standing and a dove had nested in it with her young. On this spot Amr built his mosque, the first in Egypt and **Fustat**, the City of the Tent, grew up around.

Fustat was the first of several planned developments which over the centuries contributed to the growth of the medieval city. The Nile in those days lay farther to the east along what is now Sharia el Gumhuriya which runs up into Midan Ramses where the railway station is. All of what is now modern Cairo lay then on the west bank of the river, if not beneath it. And an ancient canal, once joining the Nile with the Red Sea, lay still further to the east, along the line of Sharia Port Said, built when the canal, called the Khalig by the Arabs, was filled in during the 19th C. So the city developed along the narrow corridor of land between the canal to the west and the Moqattam Hills to the east, and extended northwards as successive rulers were intent on catching the cool summer breezes blowing in from the Mediterranean.

The Tulunid city

When Ibn Tulun, Abbasid governor of Egypt, made himself virtually independent of the Baghdad caliph in 870, he built his palace, government buildings, a hippodrome and the famous mosque bearing his name to the north of Fustat. The **Mosque of Ibn Tulun** apart, little survives of his city, and still less of Fustat. The heart of what grew into the Cairo of today was established by the Fatimids.

Cairo founded by the Fatimids

On 5 August 969, with Mars in the ascendant, the first stone of the Fatimid capital was laid to the north of the Tulunid city. The city took its name, *al-Qahira*, The Triumphant, from the warrior planet. The Fatimids, of the persistent though minority Shi'ite sect of Islam, invaded Egypt from Tunisia where their Caliphate declared its legitimacy through descent from Ali, husband of the Prophet's daughter Fatima. They imposed their Shi'ite doctrines (those same followed today in Iran) on Egypt which, apart from the Fatimid interlude, has kept within the orthodox Sunni fold. The **al-Azhar Mosque** dates from this period and is still the centre of Koranic studies for the whole Muslim world.

(Our name for the city, Cairo, derives from this al-Qahira found on maps, though as often as not Egyptians call it *Misr*. Of vague and haunting meaning, far antedating Islam, Misr is emotionally the more important name of the two and refers to both city and the country as a whole. An Egyptian abroad who says, 'I am going to Misr'. means he is returning to Egypt. If he says the same thing in Luxor, he means he is returning to Cairo. In either case, 'going to Misr' carries the sense of going home. For the fellahin, Cairo is *Misr um al-dunya*: Misr, Mother of the World.)

Saladin extends the medieval city

This walled city, centred on the popular market area known as **Khan el Khalili** and extending from the gate known as **Bab Zuwayla** in the south to **Bab al-Futuh** in the north, remains astonishingly intact both in structure and in atmosphere, the medieval city nonpareil in all the world. Its walls and area were extended by Saladin, a Kurdish general in the service of the Abbasid caliph in Baghdad. Foreign failures and the failure of the Nile itself led to the weakening of the Fatimid dynasty which trembled in confusion before the onslaught of the First Crusade. In triumphing over the armies of the West, Saladin established his own empire in Egypt and Syria and his own Ayyubid dynasty which ruled from 1171 to 1250. Orthodoxy was re-established and the Citadel begun, the redoubt of power and the centre of government throughout the troubled centuries of Mameluke and Ottoman rule.

Mameluke magnificence

Saladin's Ayyubid successors, however, relied increasingly on their slave militia, the Bahri Mamlukes. (*Mameluke* means white slave, while *bahri* means riverine and refers to their barracks on the island of Roda; these were mostly Turks and Mongols. The later Burgi Mamelukes, mostly Circassian, were quartered in the Citadel, hence *burg*.) The Mamelukes soon became an indispensable elite and successive sultans rose from their number, legitimising their authority more by the blood on their hands than the blood in their veins. The Mamelukes ruled Egypt until the Ottoman domination in 1517. In spite of the violent and repressive character of Mameluke rule, they enriched the city with their architecture, their most outstanding monuments the **Mosque of Sultan Hassan** and the **Mausoleum of Qaytbay**.

The Ottomans

Around 1300 the island of Gezira was formed as the Nile shifted westwards but the city remained largely within its old boundaries right through the Ottoman period, its architecture following traditional styles with only a few baroque exceptions inspired by the mosques of Istanbul. As a province of the Ottoman Empire, Egypt was ruled by a Turkish governor housed in the Citadel who delegated most of his authority. Though no longer providing sultans, the Mamelukes perpetuated their slave aristocracy by levees of Christian youths from the Caucasus. But their power now was chaotic and rapacious. What the Turks did not take, the Mamelukes did, and Egypt suffered from famine and disease, its population falling to two million compared to eight million in Roman times.

Napoleon and the Westernisation of Cairo

The brief French occupation of Egypt, from 1798 to 1801, was to have a profound effect on Cairo. Napoleon stayed in what was still then a country district, on the site where the old Shepheard's Hotel was later built, overlooking the Ezbekieh lake, subsequently the Ezbekieh Gardens, only recently ruined by having a main street cut through the middle and flyover amputate one side. While reorganising the government, introducing the first printing press, launching a balloon and installing windmills on the Moqattam Hills, Napoleon also planned Parisian boulevards.

When Mohammed Ali finally massacred the Mamelukes in 1811, founding a dynasty which ended only with the abdication of Farouk in 1952, he proceeded with the Westernisation of Cairo which saw the canal filled in and the great swaths of Sharia el Muski and Sharia el Qalaa (formerly Sharia Mohammed Ali) mow down long rows of the medieval city. Fortunately, however, most of the modernising of Cairo — those circles and radiating avenues you see from the air — took place on the virgin land that the Nile provided when it settled in its present bed.

Orientation
It is in this newer, Westernised part of Cairo that we can start our orientation.

Waterskiing on the Nile in Cairo

What now passes for the centre of town—for foreigners, anyway—is **Midan el Tahrir**, or Liberation Square, bounded by the Egyptian Museum to the north and the Nile Hilton to the west, with a madhouse of a bus terminus slap in the middle and a new metro station dug beneath. Hot, noisy, characterless and thick with exhaust fumes, Midan el Tahrir is among the more recent schemes to bring Cairo up to date. It was created after the 1952 revolution on the site of a British barracks, the Qasr el Nil, and at the same time powers of compulsory purchase were used to cut the **Corniche el Nil** through the many embassy and villa gardens to the south, the new roadway extending clear down to Maadi and Helwan.

South along the corniche to Garden city

A short walk along the corniche are the Semiramis Intercontinental and Shepheard's—though the famous Shepheard's Hotel of the past, whose guest list included General Gordon and Sir Richard Burton and where anyone who was anyone was seen on the terrace drinking four o'clock tea, was located near the Ezbekieh Gardens and was burnt down by demonstrators in 1952. Further south along the river is the convoluted pattern of **Garden City**, a pleasant residential district of treelined streets.

Immediately to the south of Midan el Tahrir is the Mugamaa, the suitably massive headquarters of the state administration, and next to it are the American University

9

in Cairo and the National Assembly. Going east beyond the campus and the station you come to Abdin Palace, formerly a residence of King Farouk, now partly a museum and partly the offices of the President of the Republic.

North to Midan Ramses

To the north of Midan el Tahrir, beyond the overpass leading to the new 6 October Bridge (named for the 1973 war), is the Ramses Hilton and past that the one-time slum districts of Bulaq and Shubra, now being redeveloped with skyscrapers along the river. On the corniche here is the Television Tower Building, housing radio and television studios and the press office, while the taller building beyond it is the new Ministry of Foreign Affairs. Sharia Ramses runs out from the top of Midan el Tahrir and turns northeast, leading to **Midan Ramses** with a colossal statue of Ramses II brought in 1955 from Memphis where his twin still resides. (A concrete clone has been erected on the way to the airport.) Here you will find the Mahattat Ramses or Bab el Hadeed, the main Cairo railway station for trains north to Alexandria and south to Luxor and Aswan.

Northeast to downtown

Around Midan el Tahrir and along the streets radiating out from it are numerous airline offices and travel agencies, and extending into the **downtown area** to the northeast several less expensive hotels. This downtown area is bordered by Sharia Ramses to the northwest, Sharia Tahrir to the south and Sharia el Gumhuriya to the west. Parallel to Sharia Ramses is Sharia Champollion; the Thomas Cook office is on the first street to intersect this, Sharia Mahmoud Basiony. Sharia Qasr el Nil heads more eastwards in the direction of the Ezbekieh Gardens, though not quite reaching that far; soon after leaving Midan el Tahrir you will find American Express on the right-hand side. Further on, this street intersects several others at Midan Talaat Harb. Along Sharia Talaat Harb, beginning at Midan el Tahrir and ending at Midan Orabi, are numerous shops, cinemas and eating places — also along Sharias Adli and 26 July running east-west. This is the liveliest area of modern Cairo, particularly on a Thursday night, that is preceding Friday's day of rest.

Until the creation of Midan el Tahrir, the **Ezbekieh Gardens** were the focal point for foreign visitors. The old Shepheard's Hotel stood on the corner of Sharias el Gumhuriya and Alfi at the northwest corner of the gardens, the Continental Savoy on el Gumhuriya overlooking Opera Square, which is immediately to the south of the gardens, is now a dishevelled reminder of those grand days of tourism. The Opera House mysteriously burnt down in 1971; it had been built in 1869, and the Khedive Ismail commissioned Verdi to write *Aida* to celebrate here the opening of the Suez Canal and Egypt's return to the crossroads of the world. In the event, *Aida* was late and

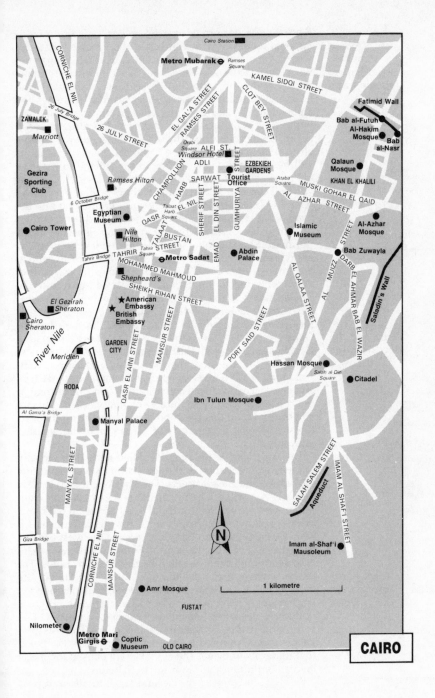

Cairo Station

Metro Mubarak ⊖ — Ramses Square

CORNICHE EL NIL

KAMEL SIDQI STREET

EL GAL'A STREET
RAMSES STREET
CLOT BEY STREET

Fatimid Wall
Bab al-Futuh
Al-Hakim Mosque
Bab al-Nasr

26 July Bridge

ZAMALEK
Marriott

26 JULY STREET

Orabi Square
Windsor Hotel
ALFI ST.
ADLI

Qalaun Mosque
KHAN EL KHALILI

Gezira Sporting Club

Ramses Hilton

6 October Bridge

CHAMPOLLION
SARWAT
HARB
EL NIL

SHERIF STREET
EL DIN STREET
GUMHURIYA STREET

Tourist Office
EZBEKIEH GARDENS
Ataba Square

MUSKI GOHAR EL QAID

AL AZHAR STREET

Cairo Tower

Egyptian Museum

Talaat Harb Square
QASR
EL BUSTAN
TALAAT HARB STREET

Nile Hilton

Tahrir Square
TAHRIR
Metro Sadat ⊖

Islamic Museum

Al-Azhar Mosque

Bab Zuwayla

DARB EL AHMAR BAB EL WAZIR

Saladin's Wall

Tahrir Bridge

MOHAMMED MAHMOUD

Abdin Palace

EMAD

AL MUIZZ STREET

El Gezirah Sheraton

Shepheard's

SHEIKH RIHAN STREET

★ American Embassy
★ British Embassy

Cairo Sheraton

Meridien

River Nile

GARDEN CITY

QASR EL AINI STREET

MANSUR STREET

PORT SAID STREET

AL QALAA STREET

Hassan Mosque
Salah al-Din Square
Citadel

RODA

Al Gama'a Bridge

Manyal Palace

Ibn Tulun Mosque

MANYAL STREET

SALAH SALEM STREET
IMAM AL SHAF'I STREET
Aqueduct

Giza Bridge

CORNICHE EL NIL

MANSUR STREET

N

Imam al-Shaf'i Mausoleum

1 kilometre

Amr Mosque

FUSTAT

Nilometer

Metro Mari Girgis ⊖
Coptic Museum

OLD CAIRO

CAIRO

Rigoletto was performed instead before a glittering international audience which included the Empress Eugénie, wife of Napoleon III. This area around Ezbekieh, though not what it used to be, is — along with the downtown area most adjacent to it — one of the best places to stay for anyone who is serious about exploring the city on foot. It enjoys the ambivalence of being on the edge of modern Cairo and within easy walking distance of the Fatimid city to the east.

The development and layout of the medieval **Islamic city** has already been outlined, and the details of its sights will be provided later. Suffice to say for the purpose of orientation that if you walk through the Ezbekieh Gardens you will come to Midan Ataba with its central post office, open 24 hours a day. From here you can press on into the heart of the bazaar area along Sharias el Muski or al-Azhar; or if instead you leave the square along Sharia al Qalaa (formerly Sharia Mohammed Ali and still called that by many) running south you come to the Islamic Museum at the intersection with Sharia Port Said, and still farther down you reach the Sultan Hassan Mosque and the Citadel. West of the Citadel is the Mosque of Ibn Tulun.

Returning again to Midan el Tahrir for bearings, there is the Tahrir Bridge which crosses the Nile to the island of **Gezira** (*gezira* is in fact Arabic for island). The central part of Gezira is taken up with the Sporting and Racing Club, next to it rising in lotus motif the 180-metre **Cairo Tower**, completed in 1962. There is an open observation deck up top, and below it an enclosed coffee lounge and a restaurant of the revolving kind. There are sweeping views of the city and beyond, and this is a good place (easy too on the feet) to establish the topography of Cairo's outlying areas in your mind.

Gezira and the
view from the
Cairo Tower

The north part of the island is called **Zamalek**, a mostly modern residential area, though with the occasional fine old home amidst leafy streets. The Marriott Hotel is located here. This part of Gezira can be reached directly from Midan Orabi along Sharia 26 July and across an old metal bridge. Following 26 July (named for the date on which King Farouk abdicated in 1952) across to the west bank of the Nile you see the suburb of **Embaba**, the site where Napoleon fought the so-called Battle of the Pyramids. Far to the north you can see the dark fan of the **Delta**. The suburb of **Heliopolis** is nearer, to the northeast, though the ancient site of Heliopolis is a bit to the north of it. There is nothing to see at the site but an Obelisk of Sesostris I (XII Dyn), and nearby at Matariya the Virgin's Tree, its predecessor much visited by medieval pilgrims in the belief that under its branches the Holy Family paused for shade before continuing their journey to Babylon.

Below you, barges, feluccas and small motor craft pass

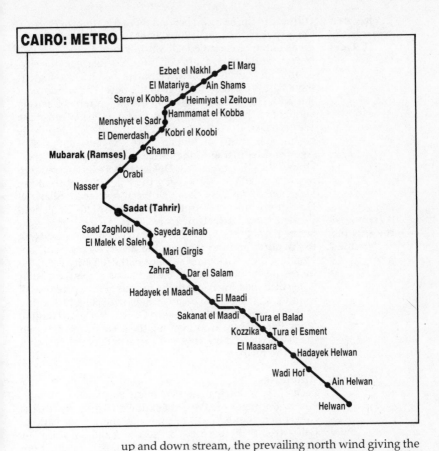

El Marg
Ezbet el Nakhl
Ain Shams
El Matariya
Heimiyat el Zeitoun
Saray el Kobba
Hammamat el Kobba
Menshyet el Sadr
Kobri el Koobi
El Demerdash
Ghamra
Mubarak (Ramses)
Orabi
Nasser
Sadat (Tahrir)
Saad Zaghloul
Sayeda Zeinab
El Malek el Saleh
Mari Girgis
Zahra
Dar el Salam
Hadayek el Maadi
El Maadi
Sakanat el Maadi
Tura el Balad
Kozzika
Tura el Esment
El Maasara
Hadayek Helwan
Wadi Hof
Ain Helwan
Helwan

View south towards Memphis

up and down stream, the prevailing north wind giving the impression by the ripples it causes on the surface of the river that the Nile flows south though of course it is flowing north, one of the few rivers in the world to do so. At the southern tip of Gezira is the El Gezirah Sheraton, while the island to the south is **Roda** with the Meridien Hotel magnificently perched like a figurehead upon its northern prow. At its southern tip is a nilometer constructed by the Ummayads in 716. About as far down but on the east bank of the Nile is **Old Cairo** with its Coptic Museum, Coptic churches and a synagogue. Much farther south is **Maadi** (along with Zamalek one of the residential areas favoured by Cairo's foreign community), and farther on still the industrial town of **Helwan**, both on the east bank. The indiscernible remains of Egypt's ancient capital, **Memphis**, lie on the west bank opposite Helwan.

Sweeping your gaze round to east and west you see how Cairo is bounded on either side by desert. The **Moqattam**

View east towards the Citadel

Hills are to the east and beyond them the Arabian Plateau. On a spur of the hills is the **Citadel**, distinguished by the dome of the Mohammed Ali Mosque, and spread before it in dark sand-brown confusion is the old quarter of the city, as though lurking in past centuries behind the higher, more lightly dusted buildings of the new. The windows of the Nile Hilton cast a silvery cubistic pattern of setting sunlight on the river. Away to the west is the plateau of the Western Desert. Along the west bank of the Nile, opposite Gezira and south of Embaba, are the new suburbs of **Agouza, Medinat el Mohandiseen** (Engineer's City) and, around the Cairo Sheraton, **Dokki**. Mrs Sadat continues to live in a villa here overlooking the Nile, just south of the hotel, once President Sadat's official residence. Sharia el Giza runs southwards from the Sheraton to the Zoological Gardens and Cairo University. This is **Giza**, here long before the suburbs began their sprawl along the west bank to the north and out towards the desert escarpment, obliterating the once extensive fields of the fellahin. From the Cairo Tower you can still make out some arable land but it is fast disappearing beneath the furious antlike progress all round you. It is best to be up in the tower at early evening as the sun sets over the Western Desert, the sharp outline of the **Pyramids** as ever marking the great divide between the distant haze of the void and the nearer ephemeral activity of the hive.

View west towards the Pyramids

Itineraries

Each of the following chapters offers an itinerary, though you might prefer breaking them down into shorter excursions or combining parts of one with another for variety. Cairo itself really deserves at least four full days of your time, and the great line of pyramids stretching along the verge of the Western Desert require another day or two. Therefore the traveller should allow himself a week in Cairo and its environs, but this may not always be possible and so under the *Practical Information* sections following each chapter the essential highlights for an abbreviated tour are listed.

PRACTICAL INFORMATION

ACCOMMODATION

Hotels in Egypt are officially rated from 5-star (luxury) to 1-star. The rating system is not always evenly graduated, and you may find that a 3-star hotel is just as good as a 4-star one, or that two 4-star hotels charge markedly different rates. Nevertheless, the official system has been used in this guide, along with a description which should help you form your own preliminary judgement.

The rates below are indicative only and

are for double rooms. They do not include taxes or other standard charges which will add 15% to your bill, nor do they include breakfast which is often obligatory. Single rooms and single occupancy of double rooms will cost about 10% less than the double room rate. Also it may be possible to get a cheaper room without bath, etc. Hotel rates in Cairo are constant year round.

Hotel bills must be paid for either in foreign currency (the better ones will accept credit cards) or in Egyptian pounds accompanied by an exchange receipt from a bank. Room rates are quoted both in US dollars and in Egyptian pounds. For convenience they are quoted here in US dollars.

5-star: $100-$160 per double room
4-star: $70 to $100 per double room
3-star: $45 to $70 per double room
2-star: $15 to $45 per double room
1-star: up to $15 per double room

Sufficient information has been provided in the list below for you to reserve in advance. Rooms at any of the international chain hotels can be booked through one of their hotels outside Egypt. Otherwise, on arrival at Cairo Airport you can go to the Tourist Information Office or Misr Travel and see if they can help. Or you can do your own hotel hunting, probably running no greater risk than having to visit a couple of hotels before finding something suitable. Often a hotel will volunteer, or can be prevailed upon, to phone ahead on your behalf, saving legwork and taxi fares.

The following is a selective list of hotels in the Cairo, Giza and Heliopolis areas:

Mena House Oberoi (5-star). Sharia al-Ahram, Giza. Tel: 855444. A historic hotel, originally a khedivial hunting lodge (converted to a hotel in 1869) and where Churchill and Roosevelt initiated the D-Day plan. 11 km from Midan el Tahrir, linked by an infrequent free hotel bus service, the Mena House is convenient rather for the Pyramids (across the road). The old wing is magnificently decorated; it is here that you should make a point of staying, especially in a room overlooking the Pyramids—for my money, *the* place to stay if you do not mind the long journey into town. A garden wing was added in 1976, pleasant but without the old style and the dramatic Pyramid views—rates here are less than 5-star. All rooms have air conditioning and colour TV. Pool, tennis, golf, casino, nightclub, business centre, car hire, travel agent, etc., make the Mena House a self-sufficient resort on the desert's edge.

Nile Hilton (5-star), Midan el Tahrir, Cairo. Tel: 740777. Right next to the Egyptian Museum and overlooking the Nile, this was the first international hotel built in Egypt (opening ceremonies in 1959 were attended by Nasser and Tito) and the first Hilton in the Middle East. It has become something of an institution. The Nile Hilton Centre, a 1981 extension, provides further rooms as well as a concentration of travel agencies, airline offices, banks, shops and business facilities in addition to those already in the main building. American Express, Avis and Egyptair are amongst those represented. It is in the main building with its larger rooms that you should try to stay, insisting on a Nile view. Pool, tennis courts, disco, nightclub, casino, sauna, plus numerous shops and a variety of eating places are amongst the facilities. The Ibis Café is open 24 hours; the Pizzeria is good; the Taverne du Champ de Mars, imported stick by stick from Brussels, is very agreeable. All rooms are air-conditioned and have colour TV.

Ramses Hilton (5-star), Corniche el Nil, Cairo. Tel: 758000. A 1981 tower, all rooms with balconies, many with a Nile view, the hotel is a short walk from the Egyptian Museum. The rooms are a bit small; all have air conditioning and colour TV. The best thing about it is its top-floor cocktail lounge with sweeping nighttime panorama. Pool, health club, casino, business centre, shops, Hertz, travel agent, etc.

Cairo Marriott (5-star), Serai el Gezira, Zamalek, Cairo. Tel: 3408888. On Gezira island overlooking the Nile, the public areas of the Marriott inhabit with effortless vulgarity an 1869 palace. The rooms are in new purpose-built towers, all air-conditioned, with colour TV. Pool, tennis courts, health club, casino, business centre, shops, car hire, travel agent, etc. Unless you like long walks, it is a taxi-ride to almost anywhere.

Cairo Sheraton (5-star), Midan el Galaa, Dokki, Cairo. Tel: 3488600. The first Sheraton in Egypt (1970), renovated in 1986, second tower opened in 1990, the hotel is located on the west bank of the Nile across the Tahrir Bridge, with upper-storey views either over the river or towards the Pyramids, all rooms air-conditioned and with colour TV. It is a lively place, with a good nightclub; also 2 pools, health club, casino, business centre, many shops, a good 24-hour café and an Avis desk.

El Gezirah Sheraton (5-star), Gezira island, Cairo. Tel: 3411333. At the southern tip of Gezira, this circular tower offers wonderful views up and down the Nile and towards the Pyramids. The service however is poor and in summer the outdoor nightclub blasts every north- and east-facing room (the ones with the best views) until 4am. Nor are its facilities up to much. This is really a rip-off group-tour oriented hotel which does not give a damn about its guests.

Meridien Le Caire (5-star), PO Box 2288, Roda island, Cairo. Tel: 845444. Access is by private bridge from the Corniche el Nil, Garden City, to the north tip of Roda from where the hotel commands a sweeping view down the Nile. French flavour: boutiques and bidets; good coffee and pastries in the 24-hour café; its Champollion Restaurant is probably the best hotel restaurant in Cairo. Pool, health centre, well-run resort-style atmosphere. All rooms soundproofed, with Nile view, air conditioning and colour TV.

Semiramis Inter-Continental (5-star), Corniche el Nil, Cairo. Tel: 3557171. On the Nile, a short walk from Midan el Tahrir, this is one of Cairo's newest (1987) luxe hotels. Its cacophonic jumble of tiered reception area cum bar cum café is a good example of how not to design a hotel, but it has a high reputation for service and is particularly favoured by businessmen. Pool, health club, business centre, shops, travel agent, car hire, etc. All rooms air-conditioned, with colour TV.

Shepheard's (5-star), Corniche el Nil, Cairo. Tel: 3553800. This is not *the* famous Shepheard's; that was near Ezbekieh Gardens and was burnt down in the nationalist riots of 1952. This was built in 1956 and has recently been refurbished. Unlike the newer 5-star hotels, it is sedate, possesses some architectural charm, and has spacious rooms. The 24-hour café is very comfortable and the top-floor bar and restaurant have good views of the river. All rooms air-conditioned and have colour TV; the preferred Nile-side rooms have ceiling to floor picture windows and balconies. Shops, travel agent, car hire, but no pool. Prices are a bit lower than at the newer 5-star hotels.

Novotel Cairo Airport (4-star), Heliopolis. Tel: 671715. Frequent courtesy buses deliver you in minutes to the airport; this, plus soundproofed rooms, a reasonable price for its range, and good facilities (including tennis court, air-conditioned rooms with colour TV), make it a practical place to stay for those facing an early-morning take-off.

Manyal Palace (4-star), Roda island, Cairo. Tel: 844687. Run by Club Méditerranée but open to all, accommodation is in bungalows in the gardens of Mohammed Ali's palace. Beautiful setting, disco, pool, air conditioning.

Flamenco (4-star), 2 Sharia El Gezira el Wasta, Zamalek, Cairo. Tel: 3400815. At the northwest end of Gezira island in a residential area, this is a Spanish-run hotel, reflected in its café and restaurant cuisine. Shops, business centre, travel agent. Air-conditioned rooms with colour TV, some with Nile views.

Atlas Zamalek (4-star), 20 Sharia Gameat el Dowal el Arabia, Mohandiseen, Cairo. Tel: 3464175. Not in Zamalek at all, but just across an arm of the Nile in the west bank residential area of Mohandiseen. Despite its distance from the centre of town, it is a popular choice, with pool, sauna, a variety of eating places. Rooms with colour TV and air-conditioning.

President (3-star), 22 Sharia Taha Hussein, Zamalek, Cairo. Tel: 3413195. In a quiet residential area of many embassies and diplomatic residences on Gezira island. Rooms are simply furnished, large and clean; all have private baths, some have TV. Bar, restaurant, and the lively Cellar Pub in the basement.

Windsor (3-star), 19 Sharia Alfi, Cairo. Tel: 915810. This is one of my favourite hotels. Early this century Baedeker ranked it just below the old Shepheard's and since then it has not changed a jot: the character is literally peeling off its walls. High-ceilinged rooms for ventilation, much old wooden furnishing, a delightful bar/lounge/dining room hung with weird curios and damaged paintings, beers served by berobed and long-dead waiters—this is the place to come for Cairo as it once was and if you are prepared to enjoy class in tatters and atmosphere in abundance. Towards Ezbekieh Gardens in downtown Cairo. Rooms with either shower or bath.

Cosmopolitan (3-star), Sharia Ibn Taalab, off Sharia Qasr el Nil, Cairo. Tel: 3923845. Tucked away in a quiet street downtown, this is an old traditional hotel nicely refurbished in 1983. Restaurant, bar, coffee shop and bank. All rooms are air-conditioned with bath.

Victoria (3-star), 66 Sharia el Gumhuriya, Cairo. Tel: 918766. A newly-renovated downtown hotel, with good food, a hairdresser and an Australian manager!

New Hotel (2-star), 21 Sharia Adli, Cairo. Tel: 3927065. Large simply-furnished and clean rooms—and clean bathrooms. Downtown.

Lotus (2-star), 12 Sharia Talaat Harb, Cairo. Tel: 750627. Opposite Felfela restaurant. Clean rooms, some with bath and air-conditioning.

Grand (2-star), 17 Sharia 26 July, Cairo. Tel: 757509. At the intersection with Talaat Harb, downtown. Clean, comfortable rooms, some with shower.

El Hussein (2-star), Midan el Hussein, Cairo. Tel: 918089. Right by the Mosque of Sayyidna al-Hussein on the edge of Khan el Khalili and with Fishawi's tea house next door, this is the best hotel for those wanting to be amidst the sights and atmosphere of Islamic Cairo. The restaurant on the roof offers a good view

of the medieval city. Rooms are clean but very simple; all are air-conditioned but only some have bathrooms.

Garden City House (1-star), 23 Sharia Kamal el Din Dalah, Cairo. Tel: 3548126. Near the Semiramis Inter-Continental, this is the best value in Cairo and one of the most popular and difficult places to get a room. It is best to write to Mme Georgetta Amato, who runs this family-style hotel, a month in advance, stating precisely your requirements and date of arrival, and specifically requesting confirmation if required. From outside there is a small sign 3 storeys up; the rooms are there and on the floor above; you take the lift. The place is well-run, clean and friendly, and the food good. Some rooms have baths, some face the river, most have balconies. There are not many single rooms. Half-board is compulsory.

Pensione Roma (1-star), 169 Sharia Imad el Din, Cairo. Tel: 911088. Near the intersection with Sharia Adli, downtown. Clean.

Hotel des Roses (1-star), 33 Sharia Talaat Harb, Cairo. Tel: 758022. Near the intersection with Sharia Sarwat, downtown. Clean rooms, some with showers; try for an upper-storey room with views.

Hostel and campsite:
Manyal Youth Hostel, 135 Sharia Abdel Aziz el-Saud, Cairo. Tel: 840729. Near the Manyal Palace on Roda island. From Midan el Tahrir, take bus 8 or 900; from Midan Ramses take bus 95. Get off at Kobri el Gamaa (University Bridge). Tolerably clean, about LE1 per night, often full up.

Camping Salome at Harraniyya, 3 km along the canal road from Giza to Saqqara. Harraniyya is the village where the late Ramses Wissa Wassef established his famous tapestry-weaving school, so the way will be well-known. Toilets, showers, meals. Camping costs about LE1.50 per night.

EATING PLACES
You can spend a fortune or a few piastres on a meal in Cairo, and choose between the world's cuisines. Not only restaurants, but coffee shops, tea rooms and snack bars are included here.

Western style food is served at all the hotels, regardless of category. Only the restaurants at a few major hotels, however, are worth going out of your way to dine at. The best is the **Champollion** at the Meridien; also worth trying are the **Rotisserie** at the Nile Hilton, **The Grill** at the El Gezira Sheraton, the **Ambassador's Club** and **The Grill** at the Semiramis and **Asia House** at Shepheard's. All are expensive. Western style meals (French International, to be exact) are also to be had at the following non-hotel restaurants:

Justine, 4 Sharia Hassan Sabri, Zamalek. Tel: 3412961. Part of the Four Corners Restaurant, the atmosphere is formal, the cuisine is nouvelle. Probably the best and most expensive restaurant in Cairo.

La Charmerie, 110 Sharia 26 July, Zamalek (set back a bit from 26 July, opposite Margaret's Boutique). Tel: 3403424. Stylish and pricey.

Don Quichotte, 9 Sharia Ahmed Heshmat, Zamalek. Tel: 3406415. Some Middle Eastern specialities. Expensive.

El Yotti, 44 Sharia Mohl el Din Abul Ezz, Mohandiseen. Tel: 3494944. Moderately priced.

It is significant that Cairo's better and newer Western style restaurants like those above are outside the downtown area which generally is deteriorating. However:

La Chesa, 21 Sharia Adli, downtown. Tel: 3939360. Operated by Swissair Restaurants, this is a haven of Swiss cleanliness, excellent food and a very good cake and pastry section.

Specialty restaurants offer one fare, with variations, though alternatives may be available:

Naniwa, Ramses Hilton Annex. Tel: 758000. Japanese in a pleasant atmosphere. Expensive.

Fu Ching, 28 Sharia Talaat Harb. Tel: 3936184. Inexpensive Chinese. Located in a passageway off Talaat Harb, downtown. Does take-aways.

Il Capo, 22 Sharia Taha Hussein, Zamalek. Tel: 3413870. Italian. Inexpensive and casual. Does take-aways. Near the President Hotel.

The Farm, 23 Maryutia Canal off Sharia al-Ahram (Pyramids Road)—signposted. Rustic setting, though fashionable. The speciality is roast lamb. Food and service are excellent. Reservations recommended. Tel: 851870. Moderately priced.

The Nile Pharaoh, a cruising restaurant got up like a pharaonic sailing barge. Lunch and dinner. Oberoi Hotels for reservations. Tel: 738855 or 738914. Expensive.

Pizzeria, Hilton Hotel, Midan el Tahrir. The atmosphere is pleasant, the food good and moderately priced.

Taverna, 3 Sharia Alfi, near Midan Orabi. Principally Cypriot, though other dishes too. Their speciality is shrimp. Inexpensive to moderate.

Oriental restaurants include the most simple peasant Egyptian through to the Levantine which can be a mixture of Egyptian, Turkish, French and other cuisines. Egypt's national dishes are *fool*, a bean paste; *tamaiya*, the same beans but pressed into a patty and fried in oil; *tahina*, a sesame paste; *babaganoush*, like tahina but eggplant instead of sesame; and *koushari*, a mixture of rice, macaroni, lentils and chickpeas, topped with a spicy sauce. Meat usually comes as kebabs and *kofta*, a spicy ground meat. The Meridien's **Le Roof** is the best of the big hotel Oriental restaurants, and is of course expensive. But you should make a point of going to local places for the local atmosphere.

Arabesque, 6 Sharia Qasr el Nil. Tel: 759869. This is an elegant downtown restaurant with a small bar; adjoining it is a gallery of Egyptian artists. The cuisine is Egyptian, Lebanese and European. Prices are moderate but imported wine will make it expensive.

Felfela, 15 Sharia Hoda Sharawi, just off Sharia Talaat Harb. Though popular with tourists and foreign residents, it is also a favourite of Egyptians and the food is certainly good and inexpensive. Tree trunks serve as tables. The specialty is fool in all its varieties of preparation, but the menu extends to meat dishes, ice creams, etc. Try the Shakshouka Felfela, a blend of ground beef, egg and spices in tomato sauce, with rice.

Al Omdah, Sharia Al-Gazair (off Sharia

18

Gameat el Dowal el Arabia), Mohandiseen. A few doors along from the Atlas Zamalek Hotel, the restaurant sign is in Arabic but features a man looking vaguely like Mark Twain. Large bowls of koushari. Cheap.

Lux, Sharia 26 July, near the intersection with Sherif, downtown. I think this was the first place I ever had an Egyptian meal. Kousharis cost next to nothing.

Khan el Khalili, 5 Sikket el Bedesfane, the main east-west street, running through the centre of Khan el Khalili. Run by Oberoi hotels and has an outdoor sitting area for coffee and tea while inside amidst oriental decor meals and mezes are served. Fairly expensive.

Abu Shakra, 69 Qasr el Aini, at the south end, about 3 km from Midan el Tahrir, near the bridge crossing over to Roda at the Manyal Palace. The epitome of its type, in marble and alabaster—also a strict Muslim establishment, serving no alcoholic beverages and closed Fridays and during Ramadan. The specialities are kofta and kebab, though sometimes pigeon and grilled chicken are also available. Usually (though not always) the food is excellent. Inexpensive to moderate.

Coffee shops, tea rooms and drink and snack bars abound, convenient for resting, cooling off and perhaps a light meal during the day:

The cafés in the major hotels have the advantage of being open 24 hours; also, they are air-conditioned. There is a minimum charge. **Le Café** at the Meridien is marvellous for its Nile views; the **lounge at Shepheard's** is a comfortable and civilised place for afternoon tea; while the Nile Hilton gets credit for its **Taverne du Champ de Mars**, a fin de siècle Brussels tavern, dismantled and reconstructed on the ground floor of the hotel. Beer, spirits and snacks are served from noon to 2am, and a reasonably priced buffet meal at evening.

Cairo Tower, Gezira island. Coffee, tea, beer, a snack are all available up top, at a slight surcharge for having got it up there, but the atmosphere is pleasant, the views wonderful.

Brazilian Coffee Shop, 38 Sharia Talaat Harb and 12 Sharia 26 July. Open from 7am to midnight, this is where to come if you care about coffee. The beans are freshly ground (unground beans can be taken away), the espresso, cappucino, café au lait—or almost any other way of drinking coffee—are excellent.

The Indian Tea Centre, off the passageway at 23 Sharia Talaat Harb. An inexpensive place where snacks are also served, though this is principally a tea room, with imported Indian teas and Indian-style pastries.

Groppi has three branches, at Midan Talaat Harb, on Sharia Adli, and in Heliopolis. It is **Garden Groppi**, as the one at the Midan el Opera end of Sharia Adli is called, that was so famous amongst British servicemen during the Second World War, and its outdoor café remains a pleasant place to sit by day or evening. There is a delicatessen here too, selling cold cuts, pastas, jams and bottles of wine.

Lappas, 17 Sharia Qasr el Nil, is a Groppi-like place of Groppi-like vintage, popular amongst those who do not want to be disturbed.

Café Riche, on Sharia Talaat Harb near the midan and next to the Brazilian Coffee Shop at No. 38, with a nondescript indoor restaurant (very cheap) and an outdoor café, frequented by Cairo's literati and where Nasser, Sadat and other officers met while planning the 1952 coup.

In wandering around the streets, either in modern or Islamic Cairo, you will encounter numerous simple establishments for having a snack, even a meal, and certainly a refreshing mint tea. There are also peripatetic street vendors, good for drinks though perhaps less so for food which may not be particularly clean. In buying anything to eat, always be sure the place has running water—if so, a modicum of hygiene can be counted upon. Forget the Cokes and 7-Ups for a change; instead pause for fresh guava, mango, orange, sugar cane or strawberry juice (after you have drunk it you scoop the strawberries from the glass with a spoon).

Finally, the café to go to when wandering round Khan el Khalili is the famous **Fishawi's** in a small alley near the

Sayyidna Hussein Mosque. Here you sit on cane chairs at marble-topped tables in a narrow passage lined with mirrors, and as coffees pass by on brass trays you are propositioned with a shoeshine, a device for making catcalls, a woman's song accompanied by a tambourine, and necklaces of jasmine flowers, their scent thick on the night air.

ENTERTAINMENT

For up-to-date listings of entertainments in Cairo, get a copy of *Cairo Today*, the city's monthly English-language magazine.

Nightclubs in the main international hotels usually offer a programme of both Oriental and Western acts, eg a first-class Egyptian belly dancer followed by some unemployed London showgirls pretending to be from Las Vegas or Paris. Fifi Abdou, however, usually puts on a one-woman show, one moment the most graceful and subtle of belly dancers, the next moment a typhoon — it is well worth finding out where she is appearing.

Some other nightclubs, like those along the Pyramids Road (Sharia al-Ahram) and a few downtown will stage a more purely Egyptian programme, and these, even if sometimes second-rate, can be delightful. A belly dancer or two will be followed by an Egyptian singer and several variety acts: human contortionists, laid back finger-cymbal players or a dull Lebanese riding a bicycle across a wire 2 metres above the stage. There is something in this of the Arab patronage of the popular mysteries, and one place to try is the **Scheherazade** at the Midan Orabi end of Sharia Alfi, downtown.

At **discos** you skip live entertainment, Western or Oriental, and twitch instead to the vibrating recorded music. Some of the best places for this are **Jackie's** at the Nile Hilton and **Regine's** (of Paris, London and New York fame) at the El Gezirah Sheraton (but both of these are open only to members or residents and their guests); also the **Saddle Room** at the Mena House Oberoi, and **After Eight**, at the end of a passageway at 6 Sharia Qasr el Nil, downtown. The food

here is very good. Closed July and August.

Casinos (admission only to non-Egyptians) are found at the Meridien, the Marriott, the Mena House, the Hiltons, the Cairo and El Gezirah Sheratons, and the Heliopolis Movenpick Hotel. Play is in US dollars, free drinks for punters, doors close at dawn.

Many events with a Western content in the **performing arts** are arranged by foreign cultural organisations:
The British Council, 192 Sharia el Nil, Agouza. Tel: 3453281.
The Goethe Institute, 5 Sharia Abdel Salam Aref. Tel: 759877.
The French Cultural Centre, 1 Sharia Madraset el Huquq el Fransia. Tel: 3553725.
The American Center, 4 Sharia Ahmed Regheb, Garden City. Tel: 3549601.
These can tell you about films, theatre and dance productions, concerts, etc, in which they are involved or know something about.
A few Egyptian activities worth knowing about:
The National Troupe and the **Reda Troupe**, both folk dance troupes, who perform regularly at the Balloon Theatre, Sharia 26 July at Sharia Nil, Agouza. Tel: 3477457.
The Arabic Music Troupe, Tel: 742864, which performs at the Gumhuria Theatre, 12 Sharia Gumhuria, downtown.
The Folkloric Orchestra of Egypt, which performs with ancient Egyptian instruments, may be found at various venues. Tel: 735153 for information.
Note that with the recent opening of the **new Opera House** (The Egyptian Education and Culture Centre) at the Gezira Exhibition Grounds on Gezira island, some of the above activities and certainly many others will now be taking place there. Contact the Tourist Office for general information.

Cinemas are mostly located around Midans Talaat Harb and Orabi, and several are likely to be showing English-language films, subtitled in Arabic. The *Egyptian Gazette* carries listings. The problem is that the Egyptians, being able to read the subtitles, do not have to listen to the dialogue. Instead the audience chatters throughout the film, which often has its sound turned down anyway, so that you will be lucky to hear much of it — perhaps not so important when considering the entertainment potential of the audience. Tickets are cheap, and all seats are reserved. You should buy your tickets several hours in advance of the performance you intend seeing, as seats go very quickly.

It is the **popular mysteries** — the man staging a backstreet show with a snake and a guinea pig or a marriage procession of loud cries and ribald song strolling down the middle of a road — that are most entertaining in Cairo. Two fixtures appealing at this level are the **Egyptian National Circus**, a good one-ring affair usually found at Agouza by the 26 July Bridge (check with the Tourist Office for details); and the **Cairo Puppet Theatre** in Midan Ataba, at the southeast end of Ezbekieh Gardens, its season from October to May, with nightly performances at 6.30 as well as Friday and Sunday shows at 11am. The puppet shows are in Arabic, which hardly matters as it is easy to follow the action, and which anyway adds to the enchantment of the productions, appealing to adults and children alike.

It is probably best to approach the son et lumière at the Pyramids on this level too, therefore so much the better if you go to the Arabic programme, not an English-language one. The **Sound and Light** show (say this to a taxi driver and you will be taken straight there) is presented twice nightly, at 7.30 and 8.30:
Monday: English/French
Tuesday: French/Italian
Wednesday: English/French
Thursday: Arabic/English
Friday: English/French
Saturday: English/Spanish
Sunday: French/German
Seating for the Sound and Light is facing the Sphinx; if you do not go by taxi, you can take the 800 or 900 bus from Midan el Tahrir, terminating at the Mena House Oberoi, and then backtrack on foot through the village at the edge of the

escarpment, a 15-minute walk — though you can shorten the hike by getting off the bus along the Pyramids Road when you see (on your left) the sign for the Sound and Light, about 1000 metres before the Mena House Hotel.

After all that high- and low-lifing, you might like some recreation. The Gezira Sporting Club admits non-members to its clay **tennis courts** and its **swimming pool**. Or go for a sundown sail in a **felucca**; these can be hired by Shepheard's Hotel.

SHOPPING
While shopping at the bazaar stalls is a matter of haggling over prices, shops and department stores in the modern part of Cairo sell at **fixed prices**. Except in shops found in the arcades of major hotels, prices are usually marked in Arabic numerals, and are often stated in piastres (100PT = LE1). So an item priced at 1000 is likely to be 1000PT or LE10. Usually, common sense will tell whether piastres or pounds is intended.

Opening hours for most shops are from 9.30 or 10am to 1 or 1.30pm, and from 4.30 or 5pm to 7.30 or 8pm, though some may remain open continuously throughout the day, particularly in Khan el Khalili. Most are closed Saturday evenings and Sundays, while some may close on Fridays. During Ramadan, shop hours are likely to be from 9.30am to 3.30pm and from 8 to 10pm or even later.

In the bazaars, price is usually what you agree on after a bout of **bargaining**. A stallkeeper will always ask more than he expects to get; the traditional response is to offer half as much. After several minutes, perhaps half an hour, a price midway between the extremes is agreed. That is the traditional way, but the visitor's impatience or foolishness can spoil the market, traders asking for and getting far more than their goods are worth. This is particularly true of hawkers at places like the Pyramids, and every now and again it is worth making a ridiculous counter-offer, perhaps only one-tenth of the asking price ... and finding it immediately accepted.

Hawkers at tourist sights are taking

advantage of their isolation and yours in demanding exorbitant amounts. The virtue of a bazaar is that there is plenty of competition. In Khan el Khalili you will find all the copperware, all the spices, all the wood and mother-of-pearl inlay, etc, in the same area, and you should browse around, examining the goods, asking the prices, getting a feel for the market. Try to be dispassionate; the more you want something the more you are likely to pay for it. A good technique is to bargain first over something you do *not* want and then casually to start bargaining over what you do want — almost as though you did not want anything and just bargained for the sport. It *is* a sport and there are rules as well as tricks of the game. Your first extreme counter-offer will be laughed at and you may feel silly; do not worry, this is part of the game. After a few offers and counter-offers, walk out. If the shop or stall owner stops you, it means he thinks there is still a deal to be made; if he does not you may have learnt you are aiming at too low a price — go back later, or go to another shop, with an adjusted view of the item's worth. The essence of a bargain, of course, is not to arrive at some formula fraction of the original asking price, but to feel that you have paid the right price, a price you could not have bettered elsewhere, a price that makes the item worth it to you.

Clothing will be found in the hotel shops, shops in the downtown area (Sharias Talaat Harb and 26 July, for example), boutiques in Zamalek, Heliopolis and downtown, and in the big department stores: **Chemla**, 11 Sharia 26 July, where low prices are more important than quality; **Cicurel**, 3 Sharia 26 July, for quality and higher prices; **Omar Effendi**, a good department store with several branches — on Sharia Talaat Harb just off Midan el Tahrir, on Sharia Adli near Sharia Talaat Harb, and also at Heliopolis and Dokki. Sizes are continental.

Shoes are found in the plethora of shoeshops along Sharia Qasr el Nil, Talaat Harb and 26 July.

The **galabiyya**, the full-length traditional garment of Egyptian men, is popular with both male and female visitors as comfortable casual wear. Fancier versions can also serve as evening wear for women. There are three basic styles: the *baladi* or peasant style, with wide sleeves and a low rounded neckline; the *saudi* style, more form-fitting, with a high-buttoned neck and cuffed sleeves; and the *efrangi* or foreign style, looking like a shirt with collar and cuffs but reaching all the way down to the floor. Several shops sell galabiyyas along Sharia Talaat Harb between Midan Talaat Harb and Sharia 26 July, and also the department stores. Fancier ones are at **Ammar**, 26 Sharia Qasr el Nil, and at **Atlas** in Khan el Khalili. Both are fixed price. Atlas is on Sikket el Badestane, the main east-west street through the bazaar. Sharia Badestan which is reached by walking north along the main Fatimid street (Sharia Muizz which goes from Bab Zuwayla to Bab al-Futuh), passing across Sharia al-Azhar and across Sharia el Muski (properly known here as Sharia Gohar el Qaid), until you see a narrow alley on your right, marked by two upright metal poles rising about a metre out of the ground: turn into it, and when it ends turn right and then left. You are now on Sharia Badestan, a main street of the bazaar, but dark and so narrow it is closed to cars. Along the left is Atlas. Mrs Sadat is known to buy her evening wear here; for all the difficulty of reaching it deep in the bazaar, the place has an international reputation.

Fabric, either for galabiyyas (Atlas and other good stores will tailor-make them for you, either from their own or your fabric) or to take home, is found in variety and quality at **Omar Effendi** (see *Clothing* above); **Salon Vert**, Sharia Qasr el Nil; or **Ouf** in el Mashhad el Hussein — heading south along Sharia Muizz and approaching Sharia al-Azhar, take the first right after Sharia el Muski/Sharia Gohar el Qaid and the first left; Ouf is on the right down this alley. Each of these stores also sell off-the-peg galabiyyas.

Weavings, carpets, tents and tapestries require further adventures if you want the best. In fact, Egypt is not particularly well-known for carpets, and if you are going to Aswan you should look around there first for small rugs and weavings. Old rugs are from time to time auctioned off, and you should look in the *Egyptian Gazette* for announcements. Carpets and rugs are found in Khan el Khalili and at **El Fatarani** and **Kazarouni**, both on Sharia Qasr el Nil.

Tent-making, on the other hand, is a Cairene speciality, and you should go to the **Street of the Tentmakers** immediately south of Bab Zuwayla. There are 6 or 7 workshops along this covered section of medieval Cairo's major north-south street, creating beautiful applique tents used at mosques or street festivals (and funerals). Some are decorated with scenes of pharaonic or Islamic themes, but the best have abstract arabesque designs or intricate calligraphy. Not that you have to buy a tent; they are made in sections and you can buy a piece about big enough to serve as a pillow cover.

Two villages outside Cairo are centres of the best tapestry-weaving in Egypt. **Harraniyya**, about 3 km along the canal road from Giza to Saqqara, was developed by the late Ramses Wissa Wassef; he taught the children how to card, dye and spin their own wool, and weave it into tapestries of their own design, usually village scenes, primitive and boldly coloured. Harraniyya's tapestries are now world-famous, and the workshop, on the right of the road, continues to be run by Wassef's wife. Tapestries cannot actually be bought here, however; for that you must go to **Senouhi**, 54 Sharia Abdel Khalek Sarwat, 5th floor, in downtown Cairo. This is also one of the best places to buy jewellery and (genuine) antiques. The other village is **Kardassa**, about 3 km off Sharia al-Ahram (turn right several hundred metres before the Mena House at the Pyramids, at the sign for Andrea's Restaurant). Here you can buy tapestries, and also bedspreads, rugs, shirts, dresses and black Bedouin dresses with bright cross-stitching — usually old, with a patchwork look after repairs, and becoming quite expensive and rare.

There are numerous **jewellery** shops in Sharia Abdel Khalek Sarwat (near Garden Groppi) and in the small street leading off it, Sikket el Manakh. And of course, there are numerous jewellers in Mouski and Khan el Khalili. By and large, Egyptian jewellery is disappointing, much of it mimicking the more obvious pharaonic motifs (cartouche, ankh, Eye of Horus), and those of Islamic motif showing little popular imagination — hands and eyes for warding off evil, or as pieces inscribed with 'Allah'. It may seem at first exotic but is limited and grows tiresome, while anything outside these two motifs is usually conceived in bad taste. **Senouhi**, 54 Sharia Abdel Khalek Sarwat, 5th floor, will have the finest selection.

Brass and copper work has long been a Cairo tradition, the standards still high today. The best place for it is in Khan el Khalili along or just off Sharia Muizz, south of the Madrasa of Qalaun. Small plates intended as ornaments and candlesticks, gongs, lamps, mugs and pitchers are the easiest to carry off — though be sure that anything you intend to drink out of is coated on the inside with another metal, like silver, as brass or copper in contact with some substances can be highly poisonous. The finest items, however, are the big brass trays which can serve as table tops (wooden stands are available).

Inlay of **wood and mother-of-pearl**, and also **leatherwork**, are also plentiful in the bazaar. Egyptian leather is not the best, however. The most common items are handbags, suitcases and hassocks. Also, more interesting than useful or comfortable, are camel saddles (for buying a camel, see below). Wooden trays, boards (including backgammon and chess boards) and boxes inlaid with mother-of-pearl and coloured bits of wood are not quite as good as those made in Syria, but are intricate and beautiful enough. Mashrabiyyas, those intricate screens found in old Cairene houses, made from bits of wood fitted together without nails or glue, occasionally come on sale in the bazaars. Muski **glass**, usually turquoise or dark brown and recognisable by its numerous air bubbles, has been handblown in Cairo since the Middle Ages, and is now turned out as ash trays, candlesticks and glasses. It is inexpensive, but also very fragile. Try Sayed Abd al Raouf, 8 Khan el Khalili. Tel: 91466. The best **nargilehs** (hubbly-bubblies) will have glass, rather than brass, bottoms. For these, try around the Street of Coppersmiths, south of the Madrasa of Qalaun.

Alabaster statuettes, also vases and scarabs, are produced and are cheapest in Luxor; **baskets** made of palm fronds are best bought in the Fayyum, though platter-shaped basketry, woven in brilliant colours, should be sought in Luxor or Aswan. **Aswan** also is excellent for woven fabrics, for ivory, ebony and spices, and indeed it has the best bazaar outside of Cairo.

Antiquities offered to you on the street are bound to be fake. Which is not to say there are not any genuine pharaonic, Coptic and Islamic artefacts around, but they will cost a lot of money and your only guarantee of their authenticity is to buy them from a shop displaying a **licence from the Department of Antiquities**. The shop will also give you a certificate of authenticity. There are several such shops in modern Cairo and in Khan el Khalili; the best is the already-mentioned **Senouhi**, 54 Sharia Abdel Khalek Sarwat, downtown. There are more shops in **Luxor**, with prices lower than in Cairo.

One of the most enjoyable excursions, whether you intend to buy or not, is to wander through the **spice market** which lies off Sharia Muizz between Sharia el Muski (Sharia Gohar el Qaid) and Sharia al-Azhar. There are bottles of perfume essences, boxes of incense and bags of herbs and spices. Also there is kohl, a black eye cosmetic. The fragrances, and the quality of the light in awninged alleyways, awaken sensation.

A similarly enjoyable excursion (though the fragrance is not the same) is to the **camel bazaar**, northwest of the city just beyond Embaba. In Arabic it is the *Souk el Gimaal*, where camel herders from the Sudan bring their animals for sale, and farmers bring their horses, donkeys, goats and other livestock. The market is every Friday and starts very early: get there by 7 or 8am. You cross over to the west bank of the Nile and head north along the corniche (Sharia el Nil), going past the 26 July Bridge until you come to a square. Here you turn left, away from the river, following Sharia Sudan for several kilometres. After a housing estate on your left (built for felaheen pouring into Cairo), a road goes off to the right across railway tracks. Take this, and immediately after crossing the tracks turn left. You will parallel a walled-in area on your right and soon meet up with people and animals heading for the market. Eventually, a road to your left crosses railway tracks again; take this and then immediately turn right. The market entrance will be on your left.

Books on Egypt and Egyptology, but also light holiday reading in paperback, are found in the major hotel bookshops, which also sell magazines and newspapers. There is also the shop in the **Egyptian Museum**. Other bookshops around town are: **Reader's Corner**, 33 Sharia Abdel Khalek Sarwat, downtown (with a branch at the Nile Hilton), has English, French and some German books, as well as old and reproduction prints (eg by David Roberts). **Lehnert and Landrock**, 44 Sharia Sherif, near Sharia Adli—English though principally German books on Egypt, while magazines and paperbacks are almost all German. They also sell (under their own imprint) the excellent Kuemmerly & Frey map of Egypt. And they do a map of Cairo, somewhat better than the one issued free by the Tourist Office, and with the virtue of a street index. **Madbouly**, Midan Talaat Harb, with English, French and some German books downstairs. Books about Egypt published by the American University in Cairo Press are obtainable at all the above shops, but you can also visit the **AUC Bookshop** at the university, 113 Sharia Qasr el Aini (entrance through Mohammed Mahmoud Gate), not far from Midan el Tahrir. Tel: 3542964.

INFORMATION
There are **Tourist Information Offices** at

the airport (Tel. 966475), downtown (head office) at 5 Sharia Adli, at the Ezbekieh end (Tel: 923000) and at the Pyramids on Sharia al-Ahram (Tel: 850259). They can provide brochures, a good free map of Cairo (with practical information on the reverse) and copies of *Cairo by Night and Day*, filled with listings of hotels, restaurants, entertainments, travel agents, embassies, etc.

The people working at their offices are charming and helpful (most helpful is the head office), but they are used to tourists going to the obvious places by the slickest means, and so have to be pressed for alternative information. If you do not want a tour, do not want to take taxis everywhere, then make it clear that you do not mind taking the local bus or train to Memphis, Saqqara, Meidum, etc, and they will come up with the information you require.

The **Tourist Police** are found browsing about ports of entry, in the bazaars and at tourist sights, and are recognised by a small blue strip on their left chest and a green armband with 'Tourist Police' written in Arabic and English. Otherwise they wear the normal police uniform, which is black in winter and white in summer. They usually speak at least 2 foreign languages and are helpful with information while doing their best to ensure that tourists are not fleeced. They are based at the airport (Tel: 965239), at the Midan Ramses railway station (Tel: 753555), at the Pyramids near the Mena House (Tel: 850259), in Midan el-Hussein on the edge of Khan el Khalili (Tel: 904827) and downtown at 5 Sharia Adli, towards Ezbekieh Gardens (Tel: 912644).

A useful source of information, as well as a brief up to date review of the news, is the *Egyptian Gazette* (published as the *Egyptian Mail* on Saturdays), Cairo's daily English-language **newspapers**. (In French there are 2 dailies. *Le Progres Egyptien* and *Journal d'Egypte*.) The *Gazette's* 'What's On' columns will tell you of current and forthcoming concerts, gallery shows, films, etc, while its 'Round and About' columns list opening times at museums and tourist sights. There are also cinema, restaurant, nightclub and travel advertisements; and television and radio listings. Also useful is the monthly English-language **magazine**, *Cairo Today*. This contains listings for entertainments, restaurants, sights, etc, while the articles will give you an in-depth look at various aspects of Cairene life. It has listings too for Alexandria.

Your own **hotel desk** or those at the major hotels, as well as such **travel agents** as Thomas Cook and American Express, and your own **embassy** can all be useful sources of varied information.

TRAVEL
The general information here on Cairo travel is supplemented by further details in subsequent chapters.

Though it is possible to get a public bus or minibus **from Cairo Airport into town** (see below), for speed, comfort and convenience (not to mention your first hairraising experience of driving in Egypt) it is close to infinitely preferable to take a limousine or taxi. Taxi drivers will be lurking in the background somewhere and it is usually possible to get a better price out of them; but you will first be presented with a rank of limousines (Mercedes and Volvos in fact) whose drivers will demand at least LE20 to anywhere in town, more to hotels out by the Pyramids. (The taxi fare *out* to the airport from town will be about LE10 to LE15.)

Taxis, which are black and white Fiats or Peugeots usually, and have meters, are in theory a cheap way of getting about within Cairo. But Cairo taxi drivers hold to an opposite theory when giving rides to tourists. Occasionally you will get into a metered taxi and the driver will actually turn the meter on, in which case you will be amazed at how cheap it is, amazed at the man's innocence, and can leave it to your conscience whether you will pay him according to the metered reading. More often than not the driver will 'forget', or say his meter is broken, or simply refuse to turn it on. You have the right to insist. In fact you will soon learn not to bother arguing or even raising the matter, and will instead devise your own rule of thumb. If say from Midan el Tahrir you go to Zamalek, Khan el Khalili or Midan Ramses (2 to 2.5 km), pay LE3. From Midan el Tahrir to Old Cairo (5 km), pay LE5. And from Midan el Tahrir to the Pyramids (11 km), pay LE10. You can feel generous in knowing you are paying well over the proper fare (and to reassure yourself, you might consider that a general in the Egyptian army earns about LE500 per month). Your driver of course will have a fit. You then make noises about calling the police. Your driver will calm down, but even if he does not, ignore him. Taking taxis in Cairo is like bargaining in Khan el Khalili; you will soon get a feel for arriving at a fare acceptable to both of you.

There are also unmetered **limousines** (Volvos and Mercedes usually) operating from the major hotels. Their fares are posted in the lobby and are fixed. Though these fares are what you are bound to pay the limousine when leaving the hotel, they can serve as a guide as to how much *less* you ought to pay the taxi driver who brings you back or takes you from one point to another during the day.

The cheapest way of getting about within and around Cairo is by **public bus**. There are the **large red and white or black and white buses** which rarely cost more than 15PT a ride. Their major terminus is in Midan el Tahrir directly in front of the Nile Hilton. They are crowded, uncomfortable, difficult to get on, even more difficult to get off of, and the main value they hold for the visitor is the entertainment derived from watching Cairenes embark and disembark through the windows. Some routes from Midan el Tahrir (indicated in Arabic numerals on the front of the bus): 8 and 900 to the Pyramids, 16 to Midan Dokki and Agouza, 400 to the airport (24-hour service on the hour), 174 to the Citadel, 600 to Zamalek.

Also there are the **small orange and white minibuses** at about 50PT a ride.

Their major terminus is also Midan el Tahrir but over towards the Mugamaa, ie near Tahrir Bridge. They are comfortable and never crowded as standing is not allowed. 24, 27 and 35 all go to Midan Ramses, while 27 goes to the airport and 82 goes to the Pyramids.

There are **river buses** too, making frequent runs from Maspero Station (on the Corniche in front of the Television Tower Building which is just north of the Ramses Hilton) clear down to Old Cairo, with stops at either side of the river along the way. There are also boats from Maspero Station north to the Nile barrages from 7am to 5pm daily.

But the great boon to visitors (not to mention Cairenes) is the completion of the new **Metro**. It is the first underground railway in Africa or the Arab world and it is excellent. For about 30PT and up, according to distance, you can travel quickly, cleanly and in comfort between important points like Midan Ramses (Metro station Mubarak), Midan el Tahrir (Sadat) and Old Cairo (Mari Girgis). Two further intersecting lines are planned.

If driving extensively in and around Cairo and farther afield, it could be worthwhile **hiring a car**. You need to be at least 25, must have an International Driver's Licence, and should have a sense of adventure: Cairenes, you will have observed, meander from one side of the road to the other as the fancy takes them, and the only way to survive is to meander with them. Both international and local car hire firms are represented; most of the major hotels will have agency desks. Avis is at the Meridien, Nile Hilton and Cairo Sheraton; Hertz at the Ramses Hilton; Europcar at the Marriott; while all these plus Budget and Inter Rent have desks at the airport and offices in town. It is worthwhile checking that everything essential actually works (like brakes) and that note is taken beforehand of any dents, etc. It is advisable to book a day in advance.

The alternative to public transport or car

hire are **tours by car or bus with guide**. There are morning, afternoon and evening tours to the Antiquities Museum, the Pyramids and Sphinx, Memphis and Saqqara, Islamic Cairo, Old Cairo, Cairo by night with night-club, etc. **Thomas Cook**, 17 Sharia Mahmoud Basiony, near Midan Talaat Harb (Tel: 743955), has a comprehensive list of tours by car with driver/guide. The more passengers, the less expensive per person. **American Express**, 15 Sharia Qasr el Nil, a short walk from Midan el Tahrir (Tel: 750444), and with branches at the Meridien, Marriott, Cairo Sheraton, and the Nile and Ramses Hiltons, does coach tours which for 1 or 2 people will work out about 40% cheaper than Cook's tours. These companies also offer **tours throughout Egypt by rail or air**.

Possibly cheaper and more comprehensive is Egypt's own tourist company **Misr Tours**, 7–9 Sharia Talaat Harb (Tel: 750010 or 750032), with an office also at 43 Qasr el Nil, and branches elsewhere. They are efficient, and can arrange accommodation, cruises, tours, and air, sea, road and rail travel.

Long-distance buses for destinations all over Egypt depart from Midan el Tahrir and Midan Ramses, and from Cairo Airport. **Share (service) taxis**, whether to the Pyramids or Alexandria or elsewhere are found in Midan el Tahrir near the Mugamaa.

The main Cairo **train station**, Mahattat Ramses, is at Midan Ramses, northeast of Midan el Tahrir. From here there are trains north into the Delta and to Alexandria, east to the Canal towns and south into Upper Egypt—Minya, Assiut, Luxor and Aswan.

Wagons-Lits carriages operate overnight to Luxor and Aswan and tickets can be bought at Ramses Station; otherwise the reservations office for Compagnie Internationale des Wagons-Lits is at 48 Sharia Giza. Tel: 3487354.

Wagons-Lits sleepers should be booked a week in advance. All first class travel should be booked at least a day in advance.

Students with an ISIC, and YHA members, can obtain a 50% reduction on rail fairs (except Wagons-Lits).

Overland travel between Egypt and Israel is by daily luxury coach; contact Travco, 13 Sharia Mahmoud Azmi, Zamalek; Tel: 3404308.

Most **airline offices** are in the vicinity of Midan el Tahrir, eg:
Air France, Midan Talaat Harb (Tel: 743516).
Air Sinai, Nile Hilton Centre (Tel: 743488).
British Airways, 1 Sharia Abdel Salam Aref, on the corner of Midan el Tahrir (Tel: 762914).
Egyptair, Nile Hilton (Tel: 750666).
El Al, 5 Sharia al Maqrizi, Zamalek (Tel: 811620).
KLM, 11 Sharia Qasr el Nil (Tel: 740717).
Lufthansa, 9 Sharia Talaat Harb (Tel: 3930366).
Olympic, 23 Sharia Qasr el Nil (Tel: 3931459).
PIA, 22 Sharia Qasr el Nil (Tel: 3924134).
SAS, 2 Sharia Champollion (Tel: 753546).
Sudan Airways, 1 Sharia el Boustan (Tel: 747398).
Swissair, 22 Sharia Qasr el Nil (Tel: 3921522).
TWA, 1 Sharia Qasr el Nil, on the corner of Midan el Tahrir (Tel: 749900).
United, 16 Sharia Adli (Tel: 3905090).

The time-honoured way of making a progress through Egypt is to **cruise along the Nile. Hilton, Sheraton** and **Oberoi** all offer year-round sailings between Luxor and Aswan, taking in Dendera and Abydos too, and usually lasting 4 nights, 5 days. Of these, the best are Oberoi for service and luxury, and Hilton for service and smallness—often the smaller the ship the more enjoyable the experience. Hilton's high season (October–May) rates are $1200 per double cabin ($700 per double cabin at low season) and include meals, sightseeing ashore, taxes and service charges. Singles and triples are also possible. Bookings can be made at the relevant hotels in Cairo or abroad.

There are an increasing number of local cruise operators, offering similar short sailings but also the full Cairo to Aswan voyage, and at rates substantially lower than those of the international hotels.

OTHER THINGS

The **Central Post Office** is at Midan el Ataba, near the Ezbekieh Gardens, and is open 24 hours daily. Other post offices are open from 8.30am to 3pm daily except Fridays. Most hotels can supply you with stamps for cards and letters. There is a good chance that post cards sent home will arrive after you do: air mail *can* take 10 days to Europe, more to the US. Mail is faster if posted at one of the luxe hotels.

To send a parcel out of Egypt requires an export licence. You must obtain this at the Central Post Office, Midan el Ataba. Go there with your parcel unwrapped; go to the third building on the left in the rear of the complex; here it will be inspected and for a small fee sewn into a cloth cover; for a further small fee you will be guided through the remaining formalities and paperwork. Your parcel must not weigh more than 20 kilos nor exceed 1.5 metres in any direction. If sending home fabrics or souvenirs you have bought, ask first at the shop whether they will do it for you. Most shops catering to tourists have export licences and are reliable.

You can **receive mail** at your hotel or care of American Express (if you have their travellers cheques or card) or care of your embassy (the envelope should be marked 'Visitors Mail') American Express will forward any mail arriving for you after your departure for LE3 or so.

Telegrams in English or French can be sent from the PTT offices on the north side of Midan el Tahrir (open 24 hours daily), or in Sharia Alfi or Sharia Adli— or from major hotels. Night letters (no service to London) cost about half as much as full rate telegrams.

Most 3- and 4-star hotels and all 5-star hotels have **telex** and **fax** services available to guests.

Local telephone calls can be made from some cigarette kiosks or from shops and restaurants—or from your hotel. **Long distance calls** can be made from major hotels or from the Midan el Tahrir (north side), Sharia Alfi or Sharia Adli PTT offices. The one at Midan el Tahrir is open 24 hours daily.

To exchange money, go to Thomas Cook, American Express, or to the banks in the major hotels—all the 5-star hotels have 24-hour banks. For a full-scale commercial banking service, there is Barclays Bank International, 12 Midan el Sheikh Youssef (PO Box 2335). Garden City, Cairo. Tel: 3549415 and 3541408.

If you have Egyptian pounds which you want to convert back into foreign currency before your departure, you can go to any bank (eg the one at the airport) and show them a receipt indicating that you had previously converted at least such an amount from foreign currency into Egyptian pounds. They will then subtract what they reckon you should have spent per day, with the result that you will probably be stuck with a load of unwanted Egyptian currency. Moral: never change too much at any one time, and what you do change, spend.

For **medical care**, ask at your hotel. Most will be able to refer you to a doctor or dentist, while some of the major hotels will have a doctor on call. Most Egyptian doctors have been trained in Europe or the US and speak English. Your embassy can also recommend doctors and dentists. In an emergency, the following private hospitals are recommended: the **Anglo-American Hospital** near the Cairo Tower, Gezira (Tel: 3418630), the **Italian Hospital** in Abbassia, northeast of Midan Ramses (Tel: 821433), and the **As Salam International Hospital**, Corniche el Nil, Maadi (Tel: 3638050). All of these are modern and fully-equipped hospitals. But note that it is unusual for any hospital to accept medical insurance: not only should you be prepared to pay cash, but a substantial deposit will be required before you are admitted.

There are several **pharmacists** around Midan el Tahrir and downtown with a wide range of medications not requiring prescriptions—describe your symptoms and, if the ailment is minor, the pharmacist will prescribe on the spot. Both imported medicines and those locally licenced are heavily subsidised by the government. You will probably be able to obtain your favourite drug at a fraction of its usual price. Cosmetics, perfumes and toilet articles are also stocked.

Your **embassy** can assist you by acting as a mail drop, advising on emergency financial and medical problems, effecting emergency communications home, etc. Embassies also encourage visitors, especially those not travelling in large groups, to register with them. It should be noted, however, that embassies cannot lend money to **stranded travellers**—though they can find ways of helping you. If stranded, you can go to Thomas Cook, American Express, Barclays International or the Nile Hilton and have them send a telegram or telex requesting your bank or persons at home to arrange the transfer of money to you in Egypt. This can be accomplished in 2-3 days. Or you can go to an airline office and ask for a pre-paid ticket, the airline cabling whomever you suggest to pay for the ticket home. Authorisation to issue you with a ticket can be received back in Cairo within 2 days.

A full list of embassies can be found in *Cairo Night and Day*; a few are listed below.

Australia, Cairo Plaza, Corniche el Nil, near the Ramses Hilton. (Tel: 777900).
Canada, 6 Sharia Mohammed Fahmi el Sayed, Garden City (Tel: 3543110).
Ireland, 3 Abu el Feda Tower, Zamalek. (Tel: 3408264).
Israel, 6 Sharia Ibn Malek, Giza (Tel: 729329).
Sudan, 3 Sharia Ibrahim, Garden City (Tel: 3545034).
United Kingdom, 7 Sharia Ahmed Raghab, Garden City (Tel: 3540850).
United States, 5 Sharia Latin America, Garden City (Tel: 3557371).

There is no **airport departure tax**. There are **banks** at the airport where you can convert your Egyptian pounds back into hard currency (lotsa luck!). The **duty-free shop**, which is available to *arriving* as well as departing passengers, sells cigarettes, tobacco, liquor, perfume, etc, but will not accept Egyptian money.

If you want a **view of the Pyramids**, sit on the right-hand side of the plane.

THE NILE, OLD CAIRO AND FUSTAT

Old Cairo and Fustat are about 5 km south of Midan el Tahrir from where you can take the metro, though you can also catch a bus, water bus or taxi (see *Practical Information* at the end of this chapter). Also there are a few places enroute worth noting for those with flexible transport. In any case, Garden City and the northern part of Roda can form a separate excursion, enjoyed on foot.

Along the Nile

A river walk The Meridien Hotel at Roda's northern tip can be reached across its own bridge from Garden City, and here you can stop for a drink and a commanding view of the Nile. Gardens run along the western bank of the island to El Gama'a Bridge which crosses over the Nile to the Zoological Gardens. From there you can walk back along the west bank of the river through Dokki, visiting the Papyrus Institute on the way, coming up to the Cairo Sheraton and so back to Midan el Tahrir via Gezira.

But a quarter of the way down Roda, its grounds overlooking the smaller eastern branch of the Nile, its entrance however facing the approach road to El Gama'a Bridge, is the **Manyal Palace**, built by Mohammed Ali. It is now a museum. On view is a reception palace, the palace proper, a private mosque and Mohammed Ali's private hunting museum, which includes a table made of elephants' ears and a hermaphrodite goat. That pretty much sets the tone of the place, which is bizarre kitsch. There is also a garden of banyan trees.

To the Nilometer Coming down the corniche from Midan el Tahrir towards Old Cairo, at a point two or three blocks south of your view across to the Manyal Palace on Roda is a traffic roundabout called **Fumm el Khalig**. This is where the canal, now covered by Sharia Port Said and its southern extension, left the river. There is a large octagonal tower of stone here, once housing great waterwheels which lifted water from the Nile to the level of the Mameluke **aqueduct** which can still be followed almost all the way to the Citadel. At this end, the aqueduct dates only from 1505 and was an extension made necessary by the westward-shifting Nile; the main part of the aqueduct, further east, was built by al-Nasr around 1311.

A further few blocks south is the Malek al-Salih bridge crossing over to the southern end of Roda. At the lower tip of the island is the **Nilometer**, dating from the 9th C, though the superstructure with its Turkish-style conical roof dates from Mohammed Ali's time. The stone-lined pit goes down well below the level of the Nile, though the water entry tunnels have been blocked up and you can descend by steps. At the centre of the pit is a graduated column for determining whether the river would rise enough, not enough, or too much, so announcing the expected fertility of all Egypt over the coming year. A reading of 16 *ells* (8.6 metres) ensured the complete irrigation of the valley; then the Nile crier would broadcast the *Wafa el Nil* or superfluity of the Nile and the dam to the Khalig would be cut amidst great festivity. The Nile used to reach its flood in mid-August, but the High Dam at Aswan now regulates its flow and it keeps a steady level year-round.

Immediately north of the Nilometer is the former Monasterly Palace, now the Centre for Art and Life.

Old Cairo

Old Cairo (*Misr el Qadima* in Arabic) describes the general area, but specifically you want to arrive at the Roman fortress (known in Arabic as *Qasr el Shamah*, Fortress of the Beacon) opposite the Mari Girgis metro station. The section of wall and two towers here formed part of the Roman **fortress of Babylon**, first built in the time of Augustus, added to by Trajan and remodelled by the Byzantines. The technique of dressed stone alternating with courses of brick is typically Roman. The portal between the towers was a water gate and excavation has revealed the original quay 6 metres below present street level, but the Nile has since shifted 400 metres to the west.

Babylon in Egypt

The Coptic Museum. Now the towers mark the entrance to the Coptic Museum, pleasantly set in gardens. It is a charming building, decorated with wooden mashrabiyyas from old Coptic houses, embracing green courtyards, airy and light within, its spirit in keeping with its collection. The exhibits cover Egypt's Christian era, from AD 300 to 1000, and are both religious and secular, linking the art of the pharaonic and Graeco-Roman periods with that of Islam. The museum is arranged in sections, covering stonework, manuscripts, textiles, icons and paintings as well as decorated ivories, woodwork, metalwork, and pottery and glass. Often, as in stone carving and painting, the work is crude, though agreeably naive. High artistic achievement, however, is found in the textiles, and there are many fine chemises, tapis and clothes here embroidered with motifs of St George, or graceful women and gazelles.

The arrangement of the museum, and some highlights: *New Wing, ground floor*:

Room 1: Pre-Christian reliefs and architectural fragments, 3rd and 4th C. The themes are pagan gods, eg Pan and Dionysos.

Room 2: Again reliefs and fragments, but of the 4th to 6th C and so early Christian. The cross is incorporated at every opportunity, often surrounded by flowers or backed by a shell forming the half-dome of a niche—see 7065, a shell with dolphins on either side. Technically the work is similar to the pre-Christian, but there is a sense of excitement at working with the new imagery—Pan and other pagan motifs had become so hackneyed.

Room 3: Reliefs and frescoes, 6th C. See 7118 showing Christ ascending to heaven in a flaming chariot. *Rooms 4 through 8* contain more of the same, including work from Abu Jeremias Monastery at Saqqara.

Room 9: Reliefs and frescoes, from the 6th through the 10th C. See 3962, 10th C Fayyum frescoes, showing Adam and Eve before and after the Fall. On the right they are naked, enjoying the fruit; on the left they clasp fig leaves to their genitals and Adam points accusingly at Eve as if to say 'You made me do it'.

Note throughout the museum the beautifully carved wood ceilings and beams.

New Wing, first floor:

Rooms 10, 11 and 12 all contain textiles, *Room 10* also displaying manuscripts and ostraka; note especially in this room, Case 5, exhibit 7948, the tapestry showing a musician and dancers (3rd–4th C), beautifully observed, fluid, rhythmic, happy. The Copts were at their best in textiles which they developed from ancient Egyptian tradition, adding to it Graeco-Roman and Sassanid influences. Plants, animals, birds and human beings blend in sumptuous decorative patterns that have a liveliness that Byzantium itself could not rival.

Room 13 contains icons and ivories; *Rooms 14, 15 and 16* display metalwork (including armour and weapons); *Room 17* has objects and several striking frescoes from Nubia.

Courtyard:

You step out from the main museum building into a courtyard like that of a grand Cairo house, planted and with mashrabiyyas round the walls. Across the court is part of the Roman wall and a gate of Babylon; you can descend to the level of the seeping Nile and step along concrete gangways beneath great arches and vaults where once were prisons, stables and a grain mill.

Old Wing:

Entered through the courtyard, the rooms here contain items of wood, pottery and glass. Most agreeable are the mashrabiyyas, fixed together without glue or nails, admitting a diffused light through their intricate Christian patterns.

Coptic churches. The oldest Coptic churches sought

security within the fortress walls, and usually they avoid facing onto the street and so are indistinguishable from neighbouring houses. Their main entrances were long ago walled up against attack, entry being through a small side door. Their plan is basilical, with a narthex or porch admitting to an aisled nave with an ikonostasis placed across the sanctuary. In seeking out the five churches within the fortress precincts, and also the synagogue, there is interest too in the winding little streets, glimpses within windows and doors, the decorations of the houses, the domes of some as in Upper Egypt, and the atmosphere of remove, of an almost rural village.

Alexandria was the Coptic Rome. Old Cairo was never a city, never a place of monuments, and it is not a ghetto. Copts live throughout Cairo and all over Egypt, and are particularly numerous in Upper Egypt. But especially within these walls it is an old and holy place, to Jews as well as Copts, and although Muslims are in the majority in Old Cairo, there are tens of thousands of Copts as well as a number of Jewish families living in the area.

The Hanging Church

The **Church of el Muallaqa**, the Hanging Church, is so named because it rests on the bastions of the southwest gate into the fortress, its nave suspended above the passage. It is reached by going out from the museum grounds between the two great towers and turning left. Though the church claims origins in the 4th C, it is unlikely that the present structure, which in any case has been rebuilt, would have been built on the walls until the Arab conquest made them redundant. Certainly, it is known to have become the seat of the patriarchate when it was moved from Alexandria to Cairo in the 11th C. The interior of El Muallaqa, with pointed arches, cedar panelling and translucent ivory screens, is intricately decorated—the carved white *marble pulpit* inlaid with marble of red and black is the finest in Egypt. Services are held in the dead Coptic language and in Arabic. On the right, as you come in, is a 10th C icon of the Virgin and Child, Egyptian faces, Byzantine crowns. On the same wall is an ancient icon of St Mark, by tradition the founder of Christianity in Egypt. El Muallaqa is dedicated to the Virgin and is properly called Sitt Mariam, St Mary. Its central sanctuary is dedicated to Christ, its left sanctuary to St George, its right sanctuary to St John the Baptist, scenes from the saints' lives decorating their iconostases.

Now walk back out to the street and turn right so that you pass by the entrance to the museum. Atop one of the Roman towers is the circular Greek Orthodox **Church of St George** (Mari Girgis) rebuilt in 1909 after a fire. It is the seat of the Greek patriarch. Further along, steps on your right lead down to a narrow street at the level of the early settlement. Walking along this, the Coptic **Convent of Mari Girgis** is on your left. Still further along, you are obliged to turn left or right. If you turn left into the narrow lane you pass (right) the Coptic **Church of Mari Girgis**, built originally in the 7th C but burnt down in the 19th, only a 14th C hall surviving. The modern church is of no interest. At the end of this lane you come to **El Adra**, the Coptic Church of the Virgin, first built in the 9th C but destroyed and rebuilt in the 18th C. It is known also as Kasriyat el Rihan, meaning pot of basil, a favoured herb of the Greek Orthodox Church. Al-Hakim's mother had been of that faith and for the duration of his reign it was transferred to Orthodox use.

If where you turned left for Al Adra you had instead turned right, you would at once be at **Abu Sarga**, the Coptic Church of St Sergius (which can also be reached by steps down from the ticket kiosk in front of the Coptic Museum). This is possibly the oldest church within the fortress, thought to date from the 5th C, though it was restored and partly rebuilt in the 12th C. European pilgrims are recorded as visiting the church from at least the 14th C because of its associations with the Flight into Egypt; steps to the right of the altar lead down to the *crypt*, once a cave, where according to tradition the Holy Family found refuge after fleeing from Herod.

Abu Sarga is typical of early Coptic churches, being a basilica with aisles separated from the nave by two rows of columns which support a high timbered roof. One column is granite, the other 11 are marble, and some bear faded paintings of the apostles, probably dating from the 8th C. Paintings of saints, probably 11th and 12th C, can also be made out within the central apse. A usual feature of early Coptic churches was a basin set in the floor of the narthex, used for Epiphany blessings. It is now boarded over. The central altar screen, inset above with ebony and ivory panels, is 13th C, but a century or so older are the carved wooden panels depicting (right) three warrior saints and (left) the Nativity and the Last Supper, probably once the leaves of a door. There is an icon in the south sanctuary of the Flight into Egypt. The marble pulpit is modern; the original rosewood pulpit and the canopied altar are now in the Coptic Museum.

Turning right out of Abu Sarga and then right at the corner, at the end of the street you see **Sitt Barbara** (St Barbara's) to the left, a synagogue to the right. The Coptic Church of Sitt Barbara was built in the 7th C to a similar pattern as Abu Sarga and like it was restored in Fatimid times. The central screen is 13th C; the icons atop it are 18th C. The marble pulpit is very fine. The relics of St Barbara are in the right-hand sanctuary; she had the misfortune to be born into the 3rd C, daughter of a pagan father, who discovering that she was a Christian, turned her over to the Roman authorities to be tortured and beheaded. Off to the left, as though an annexe, is the separate **Church of SS Cyrus and John**, also beheaded in the 3rd C.

Synagogue of Ben Ezra. This is a neighbourhood temple whose neighbourhood has gone away — left the country or gone to other parts of Cairo. It is a forlorn place, a forgotten outpost, yet it claims a more ancient history than anything else in Old Cairo.

Oldest
synagogue in
Egypt

The synagogue is the oldest in Egypt and resembles in its basilical arrangement an early Christian church. The Coptic Church of St Michael did stand here from the 4th to 9th C, but the Copts had to sell it to the Jews to pay Ibn Tulun's tax towards the erection of his mosque. Sources differ as to whether the original church was destroyed or its fabric remains in what the Rabbi of Jerusalem, Abraham Ben Ezra, at least renewed in the 12th C. But the Jews say the site has far older associations than that: here in the 6th C BC Jeremiah preached after Nebuchadnezzar's destruction of Jerusalem, and it was the presence of their community here, they say, that drew the Holy Family to Babylon. For the same reason, say the Copts, the apostles Peter and Mark came here, in proof of this citing I Peter 5:13: 'The church that is at Babylon elected together with you, saluteth you; and so doth Marcus my son'. The rest of Christendom argues that Babylon is here a metaphor for Rome; but there is the suspicion that this interpretation is ingenuous, serving to appropriate Peter to Rome in order there to crown him pope and martyr, legitimating the Vatican's claim to apostolic supremacy.

Ben Ezra's synagogue sits in a small shady garden, its exterior plain, a Star of David in wrought iron over the gate. Inside there is an arch of ablaq masonry and a small stained-glass window towards the far end above the sort of intricate stone inlay work you would expect to see around the mihrab of a mosque. The synagogue is undergoing extensive restoration, paid for by the Egyptian government and foreign donors.

Nathan Abraham Moishe Cohen lives opposite, and is often found sitting outside passing the time with his friend Ahmed. Since at least 1967 when I first came to this synagogue, Rabbi Cohen (who must be a rabbi by default, as he is illiterate) has been selling charmingly awful postcards of himself at wickedly high prices. Buy one and he may show you exactly where pharaoh's daughter plucked Moses from the bullrushes (I would have mistaken it for a sewer), the Miracle Rock beneath which Jeremiah is supposed to be buried, and tell you how the synagogue

Moses in the
bullrushes

once possessed a library of 100,000 books, all gone. Discovered hidden in a genizah in the walls at the end of the 19th C was an ancient Torah, now dispersed throughout the great libraries of the Western world.

Turning right out of the synagogue gate, a lane passes an abandoned Jewish school on the right and leads into a **Coptic cemetery**, a complete town of bungalows for the dead.

Fustat

Emerging from the garden of the Coptic Museum, or back up the steps from the warren of streets where you have been visiting churches within the fortress walls, turn right (that is walk two or three blocks north of the fortress with the railway line on your left) and you will come to the **Mosque of Amr**, so restored and expanded that nothing remains of the original built here in 642, the first mosque in Egypt and the point from which the country's conversion to Islam began. Except for its associations, the present mosque is without interest. Its dimensions date to 827 when it was doubled in size, and it has several times since been restored, and has recently been restored again. It is a pedestrian reminder of a cheaply won victory, and you pause to wonder what it would take to reverse the effect of Amr's 3500 men.

Behind the mosque extends what appears to be a vast and smoking rubbish dump. The curious should wander into its midst — and be amazed and rewarded with one of the most fascinating sights in Cairo. No smouldering heaps at all, but a **community of earthenware manufacturers** whose seemingly rubbish houses (you should be careful not to fall through their ceilings as you walk over them) stand, or settle, amidst a complete and complex process for the making of fine clay and the fashioning of narghile stems, drums, small pots, large amphoras and road-sized drainage pipes — indeed these people could equip a band, a kitchen or a city, and do probably meet the earthenware needs of a large part of Cairo.

There are vats dug into the ground for mixing and refining clay, subterranean workshops where potters draw from shapeless lumps beautifully curved vessels with all the mastery and mystery of a fakir charming a thick brown snake, and there are enormous beehive kilns like Mycenaean tombs fired from below with mounds of wood shavings shovelled in by Beelzebub children.

At evening these mud-covered people wash themselves off, the women appear from out of their hovels in bright dresses, flowers are arranged in soft-drink bottles, a television — wired up to a car battery — is switched on, tea is made, chairs set out, and if you are there then you will be invited to join them in watching the setting sun.

Synagogue of Ben Ezra, Old Cairo

The true beginnings of Cairo

Beyond this potters community—or, more easily, by returning towards the fortress of Babylon but turning left up the road running alongside the cemetery wall—lie the dismal **remains of Fustat**, that is the foundations and lower walls of the first Arab city in Egypt, the true beginnings of Cairo. Once famous for its glassware and ceramics, with water supply and sanitation facilities far more advanced than anything in Europe until the 18th C, the city was destroyed and abandoned in 1168 rather than let it fall into the hands of the Christian king of Jerusalem. It is not at Amr's mosque but here amidst this wreckage that you feel something of the spirit of Arab Egypt: a people brave and confident enough to destroy their finest creations to deny succour to their enemy, to fight another day and win and rebuild, filling their new city of Cairo which you can see rising to the north with some of the greatest monuments of medieval civilisation.

PRACTICAL INFORMATION

Details for visiting Old Cairo and Fustat follow later, but first some information on points of interest **along the Nile** which can all be easily reached on foot from Midan el Tahrir.

The Cairo Tower on the island of Gezira rises 187 metres and offers marvellous panoramas from its 14th level restaurant, 15th level cafeteria and 16th level observation platform. Fee for the ascent.

The Ethnological Museum, Sharia Qasr el Aini, a few blocks south of Midan el Tahrir. Open 9am to 1pm daily, closed Friday. Free. A small museum with displays of traditional village handicrafts and costumes from all over Egypt.

The Manyal Palace on the island of Roda is open daily from 9am to 2pm. LE1 entry.

The Papyrus Institute, on a houseboat tied up along Sharia el Nil, is just south of the Cairo Sheraton in Giza. Open from 10am to 7pm daily, free. Founded by Prof. Hassan Ragab, this is a workshop, research centre and small museum demonstrating the manufacture and use of this first flexible writing material. Only *cyperus papyrus*, the same plant used by the ancients, is used here (the institute has several commercial imita-

tors, but they use the modern *cyperus alopecuroides* of inferior quality). The institute grows at least some of its own papyrus, and exhibits copies of ancient papyri and sells others. (As you go down the quayside steps, notice on your left the plaque marking the highest level of the Nile during the flood of September 1887.)

The Agricultural Museum and the **Cotton Museum**, next to each other off Sharia Abdel Aziz Radwan, near the exit of the 6 October Bridge in Dokki. Open from 9am to 2pm except Fridays when they close at noon; closed Mondays. Small fee. The Agricultural Museum displays all aspects of present Egyptian rural life, while the Cotton Museum concentrates on the country's single most important crop.

If taking a **taxi** to the Fortress of Babylon in Old Cairo, ask first for *Misr* (or *Masr*) *el Qadima*, ie Old Cairo, and then specify *Mari Girgis*, ie St George, and he will bring you right to the walls outside the Coptic Museum. By **Metro**, get off at Mari Girgis station; by **river bus** the landing stage is also called Mari Girgis.

The churches close at 4pm; the

synagogue keeps irregular hours and usually Rabbi Cohen or Ahmed are there after 4pm to show you around. All are free but are anxious for donations.

The Coptic Museum is open from 9am to 4pm daily except Fridays when it closes between 11am and 1pm. LE3 entry **fee**. Bags and cameras must be checked (no fee), though you can take your camera in by paying a special fee.

An **abbreviated tour** of the places mentioned in this chapter should at least include the Coptic Museum.

TOURING ISLAMIC CAIRO

Islam in Egypt began at Fustat (previous chapter) and flowered into a great civilisation, many of whose most beautiful monuments survive throughout the medieval quarters of Cairo. The following six chapters tour this Islamic Cairo, progressing generally from south to north.

The method   The Islamic monuments of Cairo, and there are hundreds of them, are each marked with a small green enamelled plaque bearing an Arabic number. These numbers are given after the name of each monument covered in the itineraries of the following chapters to ensure identification. Although these are historical monuments, they are often places of current worship and when touring this most conservative part of the city you should dress and act with decorum. Women should not wear short dresses or too-revealing blouses. Inside mosques you must remove your shoes, or shoe coverings will be provided. For this, and if you accept the services of a guide, or sometimes if you ask to be shown the way up a minaret, baksheesh will be expected. And there is also an entry fee to many of the monuments. In short, it is a good idea to carry around a lot of small change.

You may sometimes find yourself in a mosque at prayer time, and then, though visitors are otherwise welcome, you might be asked to retreat into an alcove or out onto the street. Normally though the atmosphere is relaxed, even to the point where many of Mohammed's precepts on mosque conduct are ignored. Egypt in this as in many other ways is more liberal than most other Muslim countries.

Comfortable walking shoes are recommended. Though you might rely on a taxi or other transport to get you to the beginning of the itinerary or to some of the major monuments along the route, walking is otherwise preferable for a sense of leisure and atmosphere, and also because some places are difficult to get at or to discover even once you are in the vicinity. There are numerous *kahwehs* along the way, that is places to sit—often just a few chairs beneath the shade of a tree or awning—for a coffee or more likely a refreshing cup of mint tea. Then there is immediate tranquillity; you give your feet a rest and let the city parade by before you.

The grandeur of Islam   In the 14th C the great Arab historian Ibn Khaldun wrote that 'he who has not seen Cairo cannot know the grandeur of Islam. It is the metropolis of the universe, the garden of the world, the nest of the human species, the gateway to Islam, the throne of royalty: it is a city embellished with castles and palaces and adorned with monasteries of

40

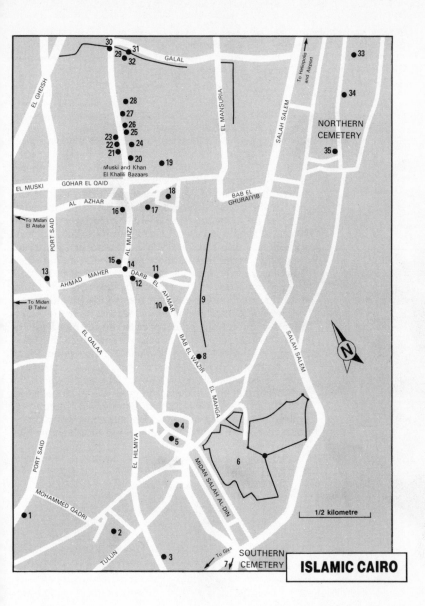

ISLAMIC CAIRO

1. Mosque of Sayyida Zeinab	4. Rifa'i Mosque	9. Saladin's Walls
	5. Mosque of Sultan Hassan	10. Maridani Mosque
2. Mosque of Ibn Tulun and the Gayer-Anderson House	6. The Citadel	11. Qijmas al-Ishaqi Mosque
	7. Mausoleum of Imam al-Shaf'i	12. Mosque of Salih Talai
3. Tomb of Shagarat al-Durr	8. Aqsunqur (Blue) Mosque	13. Islamic Museum and Egyptian Library
		14. Bab Zuwayla

dervishes and with colleges lit by the moons and the stars of erudition'. Along with Cordoba and Baghdad, it was one of the great centres of the Arab world, but while Cordoba fell to the *Reconquista* and Baghdad was destroyed by the Mongols, medieval Cairo survives. The erudition Ibn Khaldun refers to was more the Muslim version of how many angels could dance upon the head of a pin, but otherwise many of the marvels he describes still wait for you, often so unobtrusively that you could pass a facade a hundred times and never guess at the grandeur within.

After sometimes centuries of neglect, there is a new Egyptian and international appreciation of Cairo's Islamic monuments, and a recent drive is very ably restoring these treasures. The streets may be ancient, narrow and dusty, full of strange colour and smell. People may be curious, children occasionally a nuisance and merchants in the tourist bazaars importunate, but generally the inhabitants of these quarters, like Egyptians throughout the country, will be friendly and helpful. This is the heart of Cairo, a heart that anyone with the least sense of adventure will come to love.

AROUND THE CITADEL

If you have time to visit only one Islamic monument, the **Mosque of Ibn Tulun** (220) should be your choice. The mosque can be reached by going east from Midan al-Sayyida Zeinab at the bottom of Sharia Port Said or west from Midan Salah al-Din below the Citadel. The area, though not ancient, is poor and rundown, but behind its outer courtyard or *ziyadah* the mosque achieves an isolation which heightens the dramatic effect of the inner courtyard's bold simplicity.

Congregational plan

Ibn Tulun was sent to govern Cairo by the Abbassid caliph at Bagdad and the mosque, built in 876-9, displays strong Mesopotamian influence. A congregational mosque with an inner courtyard or *sahn* of parade ground proportions, it strives to fulfil the ideal of accommodating all the troops and subjects of the fortress capital for Friday prayers. Arcades run round the sahn on four sides, deeper along the qibla wall facing Mecca. Brick piers support the pointed horseshoe arches which have a slight return, that is they continue their curve inwards at the bottom, and the arches are decorated with carved stucco (restored on the outer arches but original on the others within the arcades), a technique Ibn Tulun introduced to Cairo. The windows along the qibla wall (to your left as you enter the mosque) have stucco grilles (the fifth and sixth from the left are original), permitting a faint light into this deeper arcade with its prayer niche or *mihrab* and beautifully carved pulpit or *minbar*, 13th C restorations. The roof, like the repaired stucco work, is owed to the efforts of 20th C restorers. Original, however, is the Koranic inscription carved in sycamore running at a height round the interior of the four arcades.

The effect as you enter the sahn is of severe simplicity, yet these details of carved stucco and sycamore and returning arches offer subtle relief. You should walk round the sahn under the arcades to appreciate the play that is made with light and shadows, the rhythm of the arches, the harmony of the ensemble.

At the centre of the sahn is a 13th C fountain. All these 13th C restorations and additions were undertaken by Sultan Lajin who had assassinated the incumbent sultan and hid in the then decrepit mosque. He vowed that if he survived to be raised to the sultnate he would restore his hideaway, and to him belongs an explanation also for the striking *minaret* opposite the qibla wall. The original was Tulun's, in the form of spiral, and there is a story of Tulun, normally of grave demeanor, absentmindedly twiddling a strip of paper round his finger to the consternation of his audience, excusing himself with the explanation that it was the model for his new minaret. In fact its prototype, still standing, was the minaret of the Great Mosque of Samarra in Iraq. But Lajin had to rebuild it and out of taste or for stability gave it a squared base. It succeeds in being extraordinary and along with the merlons along the parapets of the arcades, like a paperchain of cut-out men, it has the alertness of the surreal. You can climb the minaret right to the top, though as you round the spiral there is nothing to steady you and a high breeze adds to the vertigo. There is nothing much close by but tenements with views into bedroom windows, though to the west you can see the Pyramids, to the north pick out the major landmarks of the Fatimid city, and below you again the forthright plan of mosque.

At the northeast corner of the Ibn Tulun Mosque is the Bayt al-Kritliyya, the House of the Cretan Woman, though in fact it is two 17th C houses knocked together. It is better known as the **Gayer-Anderson House**, named for the British major who restored and occupied it earlier this century, filling it with his eclectic collection of English, French and oriental furniture and bric-a-brac which can be disconcertingly anachronistic, but does give the place a lived-in feeling. Its tourist reputation must be founded on this, and its proximity to the Ibn Tulun, for otherwise it is not half as fine as the Bayt al-Suhaymi mentioned in a later chapter.

The harem   Overlooking its large reception room is a balcony enclosed in a wooden mashrabiyya screen from which the women of the harem could discreetly observe male visitors and their entertainments. Lane in his *Manners and Customs of the Modern Egyptians*, which describes Cairo in the 1830s, says the women 'have the character of being the most licentious in their feelings of all females who lay any claim to be considered as members of a civilised nation ... What liberty they have, many of them, it is said, abuse; and most of them are not considered safe unless under lock and key, to which restraint few are subjected. It is believed that they possess a degree of cunning in the management of their intrigues that the most prudent and careful husband cannot guard against'. Indeed, Lane believed that Egyptian women were under less restraint than those in any other country of the Turkish empire, with those 'of the lower orders flirting and jesting with men in public, and men laying their hands upon them very freely'. As for those of the upper classes: 'They generally look upon restraint with a degree of pride, as evincing the husband's care for them and value themselves upon their being hidden as treasures'. The only man allowed into the harem, that is the female domestic quarters, was the husband—and so the strictures worked against men, too, the only unveiled women they could see being their wives or female slaves.

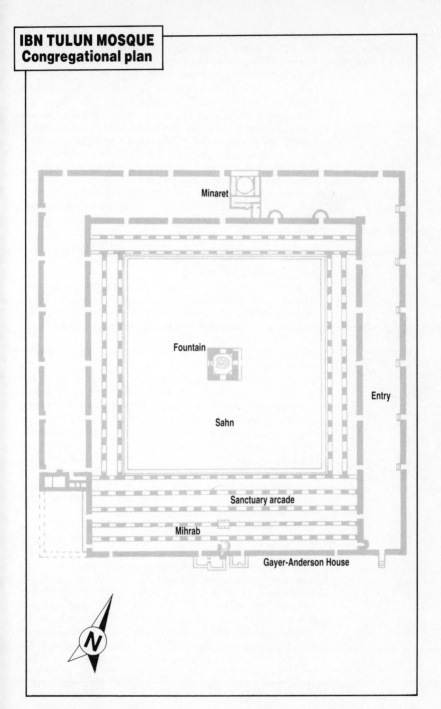

IBN TULUN MOSQUE
Congregational plan

Minaret

Fountain

Sahn

Entry

Sanctuary arcade

Mihrab

Gayer-Anderson House

N

Shagarat al-Durr

Those interested in making a romantic pilgrimage to the
Tomb of Shagarat al-Durr should walk southwards along
the medieval city's main street, here called Sharia al-
Ashraf, which passes just to the east of Ibn Tulun's
mosque. The tomb (169) is at the edge of the Southern
Cemetery in one of Cairo's poorest areas. Built in 1250, it is
small and simple, though in allusion to her name, Tree of
Pearls, the prayer niche inside bears fine Byzantine-style
mosaics of the tree of life inlaid with mother-of-pearl. She
and a near-contemporary at Delhi have been the only two
female Muslim sovereigns; Benazir Bhutto joined them as
only the third Muslim woman ruler in history. It is a
dangerous game and Shagarat al-Durr played it fast and
loose, coming to a sticky end: only part of her body lies
within her tomb—the rest was eaten by the dogs. Her story
is told in the chapter *To the Northern Walls*.

Midan Salah al-Din

Walk to Midan Salah al-Din; to your left (north) are two
large mosques pressed against each other like the walls of a
canyon, Sharia el Qalaa cutting between them. The
mosque on the right is the **Rifa'i**, a modern imitation of
Bahri Mameluke style, where members of the late royal
family, including King Farouk, are buried—and now also
the ex-Shah of Iran. The best thing about the Rifa'i is its
near-abutment with the Mosque of Sultan Hassan on the
left, the canyon enhancing the massiveness of the latter.
Both mosques are lit by orange lights at night, as though
the light itself was old, not bright and white, and had been
lingering on the facades for some long time until it dark-
ened with age. But then in the darkness is the booming call
to evening prayer, not mysterious but electrically
amplified, saving the muezzin not only his voice but the
long trudge up to the top of the minaret. This is one slip
from fundamentalist practice, prevalent now throughout
the Middle East, which is to be regretted.

The Mosque-madrasa of Sultan Hassan (133) is
genuinely of the Bahri Mameluke period and was built—of
stone (reputedly from the Great Pyramid), unlike the brick
of Tulunid and some Fatimid mosques—in 1356–63. Its
short distance from the Mosque of Ibn Tulun allows a ready
comparison between these exemplars of the two principal
forms of Cairo mosque. The purpose of the congregational
is to gather in and architecturally the emphasis is on the
rectangular and the horizontal. But the Sultan Hassan
served as a theological school, a *madrasa*. The madrasa was
first introduced to Egypt by Saladin as part of his effort
to combat and suppress the Fatimid Shi'ites. Class and
dormitory space required a vertical structure, most

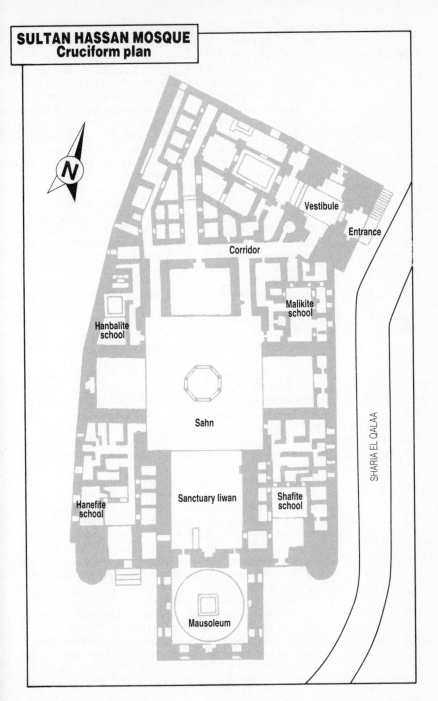

SULTAN HASSAN MOSQUE
Cruciform plan

N

Vestibule

Entrance

Corridor

Malikite school

Hanbalite school

Sahn

Sanctuary liwan

Shafite school

Hanefite school

SHARIA EL QALAA

Mausoleum

functionally a cube. The central courtyard remains a feature, but opening onto each of its sides are four enormous vaulted halls or *liwans*, creating a cruciform plan. The doctrinal justification for four liwans was that each served as a place for teaching one of the four Sunni, that is orthodox, Muslim rites (Shafite, Malikite, Hanefite and Hanbalite), though the origins of the liwan are found at Hatra in Iraq, an Arab city flourishing at least 400 years before Mohammed. But it was the Mamelukes who arranged them with magnificent effect in cruciform plan and who also added to their mosque-madrasas domed mausolea. Hassan's mausoleum is appended to the south end of the mosque but his tomb is empty; he was executed two years before its completion and his body disappeared.

Cruciform plan

There are many who regard the Sultan Hassan as the outstanding Islamic monument in Egypt, and certainly it vies with the Ibn Tulun. Though entirely different in type, the two mosques share a boldness of conception and clarity of execution, gathering still more strength in restraining decoration to the minimum necessary solely to underline architectural form. There is self-confidence, and at the Sultan Hassan even architectural insolence, but rarely indulgence.

The Sultan Hassan already impresses from the outside. Though it stands beneath the glare of the Citadel it holds its own, its great cornice and the strong verticals of its facade rising to the challenge. Notice how the broad surfaces along the east and west sides are relieved by blind recesses into which the paired arch windows of the dormitories are set. Height is especially emphasised as you enter on Sharia el Qalaa the towering *portal with its stalactite decorations*—a favourite Marmeluke motif. The portal is at an angle to the main east flank of the mosque and the west flank too is bent, though at first sight the building had seemed more regular. Earlier periods had enjoyed more space, but as Cairo grew and became more dense the Mamelukes had to squeeze their buildings in where they could, though they had a fetish for achieving a cubistic effect no matter how irregular the plot. The liwans had also to be cruciform regardless of the exterior and in the Sultan Hassan this has been neatly done, all hint inside of the irregularity of the outer walls suppressed except for the slight angle of the door in the west liwan.

Characteristics of Mameluke architecture

The portal leads to a domed cruciform vestibule and you turn left into a dark angled passage. It empties suddenly into the north end of the brilliantly sun-filled sahn, certainly a deliberate effect and a preparation for the play of light and shadow, concrete and void, intended for the courtyard and its liwans. It is important that you do not come too late in the day, indeed it is best that you visit the

Mosque of Sultan Hassan: soaring liwans

Sultan Hassan in the morning when the sun lights up the mausoleum and west liwan and begins its long and rarely accomplished reach into the full depth of the sahn. Its depth is considerable, for the liwans lift about as high as the sahn is long. The sun soon passes, illuminating hardly more than the merlons by late afternoon, and much of the architectural effect of direct sunlight and strong shadows is lost so that the mosque can then seem a disappointment. The stucco anyway is pasty brown with sand and dirt, and other details need cleaning.

The gazebo at the centre of the sahn has been rebuilt in Ottoman style and is used now for ablutions. The original fountain is met later on in this guide at the Maridani Mosque. Hundreds of chains hang down from the liwans, the glow of their oil lamps at night a delight reserved for the imagination as they are all gone, though some can be seen in the Islamic Museum. The *sanctuary liwan* is opposite the entrance passage, a Kufic band running within it and an unfortunately fussy marble decoration on its qibla wall. The columns on either side of the mihrab are from some Christian edifice, possibly Crusader—they do not seem Byzantine. Farther to either side of the mihrab are doors leading into the *mausoleum*. The right-hand door is panelled

49

with original bronze inlaid with gold and dazzles when polished. The mausoleum dome collapsed in the 17th C and was rebuilt in the 18th C in the lofty imperial style of Istanbul, though it rests on the original stalactite squinches. Rich though the restored decorations are, the atmosphere is sombre and Hassan's cenotaph, surrounded by a wooden screen where women pray for the sultan's intercession, is very simple. From the grilled windows there are views of the Citadel.

Visiting the Citadel

Returning towards the Citadel you once more enter Midan Salah al-Din, extended by clearances at the instruction of General Kitchener. It was here that the annual pilgrimage to Mecca gathered before winding through streets lined with thousands of spectators and leaving the city at the northern Fatimid gates of Bab al-Futuh and Bab al-Nasr. The long park to its south was a parade ground and polo field for the Mamelukes. Up a ramp at the front of the Citadel is a gate, closed to the public, **Bab al-Azab**. The crooked lane behind the gate, enclosed by high walls, was the scene of the massacre of the Mamelukes by Mohammed Ali in 1811. Only one escaped, leaping on horseback through a gap in the wall into a moat. During the Ottoman occupation and even under Napoleon the Mamelukes had survived and were a power to be reckoned with. Mohammed Ali invited them to dinner at the Citadel, bidding them homewards via this cul-de-sac and cutting them down with their bellies full.

The entry to the Citadel is round to the left, that is clockwise round its base. There is another entrance round the rear, off the Heliopolis and airport road. Much of the Citadel is off-limits, reserved for the military, an echo of its role as stronghold of the city from the time Saladin in 1176 built his fortress here to the reign of Mohammed Ali. For almost 700 years nearly all Egypt's rulers lived in the Citadel, held court, dispensed justice and received ambassadors. A succession of palaces and elaborate buildings thrown up during the Mameluke period were mostly levelled by Mohammed Ali when he built his mosque and **Bijou Palace** in their place. The palace, to the south of the mosque, is now a museum housing objects of its era and makes a pleasant visit if you have the time.

The Mosque of Mohammed Ali, a Turkish delight on the Cairo skyline, proves disappointing close up—though perhaps not for those who have never visited an imperial Ottoman mosque in Turkey. Half domes rise as buttresses for the high central dome and the two thin minarets add an ethereal touch, more in tune perhaps with our Oriental dreams than the robust Arab minarets of Cairo. But the

Massacre of the Mamelukes

Turkish delight

alabaster cladding, a gesture of baroque luxe, has cheapened with time, while the pretty courtyard with its gingerbread *clock* (given by Louis Philippe in exchange for the obelisk in the Place de la Concorde), suggests a folly rigged up for fashion and amusement. That could explain why the mosque is so popular with tourists, for also the interior is vast and agreeably cool, the dome huge and the decorations in opulent bad taste. Principally, though, the architecture is routine; there is no feeling of lift or weight-lessness to the dome that you find in the better Istanbul mosques, nor an appeal to spiritual contemplation. Mohammed Ali, whose *tomb* is on the right as you enter, meant this more as a symbol of the Ottoman power he had snatched.

From the parapet to the southwest there is a good view of the mosques of Hassan and Tulun and a panorama of the city which will be more or less impressive depending on the cinereous haze that heat and Helwan together smother Cairo with.

Across from the entrance to the courtyard of the Moham-med Ali Mosque is the **Mosque of al-Nasr Mohammed** (143), not much visited, dating from 1318-35. Once the principal mosque of the Citadel, it was built in the congre-gational style with an arcaded courtyard, many of the columns re-used from pharaonic, Roman and Byzantine buildings. Plain though it is outside, it is beautiful inside, all the more so as Turkish vandals stripped it of its marble panels, revealing its simple elegance. The two minarets are unique for the pincushion shape of their tops and their Mongol-inspired faience decoration, of which only traces remain.

On leaving the Mosque of al-Nasr, turn tight and go round it, then take the first road to the right on the east side of the mosque. This brings you to a tower which stands over **Yusuf's (or Joseph's) Well** (305), also known as Salah al-Din's Well or Dir al-Halazun, the Well of the Snail for the spiral staircase leading 88 metres down the great central shaft to the level of the Nile. (The descent can be danger-ous.) Yusuf was one of Saladin's names and the well was dug during his time by Crusader prisoners, providing a secure source of water in case of siege. The water reaches the well by natural rather than artificial channels, and was brought up by donkeys, the rock steps covered with earth to provide them with a foothold.

The Southern Cemetery
At this point you can interrupt your progress north with a visit to the Southern Cemetery, a vast, confusing and dilapidated Muslim necropolis stretching as far as Maadi. The Northern Cemetery generally offers the more

impressive monuments and will be covered in a later chapter. But if you avail yourself of transport (or make the long walk there and back), the **Mausoleum of Imam al-Shaf'i** (281) in the Southern Cemetery would more than repay an excursion.

The mausoleum is most easily reached by heading south from the Citadel along the street bearing the Imam's name, a distance of about 2 km from Midan Salah al-Din. A descendant of an uncle of the Prophet, al-Shaf'i was the founder of one of the four rites of Sunni Islam and died in 820. The cenotaph was put here by Saladin and the mausoleum built by his brother-successor's wife who is also buried here. The mausoleum is covered by a large wooden dome sheathed in lead and is the largest Islamic mortuary chamber in Egypt. Inside, a couple of cats, some birds

Magnificent dome

chirping, men lying about or reading the Koran, and above this the magnificent dome painted red and blue and gold, a pattern of flowers rising to the highest sound of birdsong. The original lighting system of lamps suspended from carved beams is intact—the only such in Cairo.

The spot itself is of significance: it was here that Saladin founded the first madrasa in Egypt to counter the Fatimid heresy, and it became a centre of Shafite missionary work, the rite predominant even today in southern Arabia, Bahrain, Malaysia and East Africa. The majority of Cairenes, too, are Shafites, and as the Imam is revered as one of the great Muslim saints (achieved by popular acclamation, as there is no formal notion of sainthood in Islam), the mausoleum is annually—in the eighth month of the Muslim calendar, lasting for a week from, usually, the first Wednesday—the site of great *moulid*, an anniversary birthday festival, in honour of Shaf'i. Atop the dome, like a weathervane, is a metal boat in which there used to be placed on the occasion of the moulid about 150 kilos of wheat and a camel-load of water for the birds. The boat is said to turn sometimes when there is no wind to move it, and according to the position it takes to foretoken various events, good or evil, such as plenty or scarcity, or the death of some great man.

PRACTICAL INFORMATION

To reach the starting point of this tour you can take a **taxi** or you can ride to Midan Salah al-Din (lying between the Citadel and the Sultan Hassan Mosque) on the **No. 72 bus** or the **No. 54 minibus** from Midan el Tahrir. All the monuments in this chapter are quite close together with the exception of the Mausoleum of Imam al-Shaf'i—to reach this take the **No. 405 bus** south from Midan Salah al-Shaf'i; it then turns left towards the Moqattam Hills and just where it does so there is a bus stop. You then walk down Sharia Imam al-Shaf'i a few hundred metres. Or take the **tram** from Midan Salah al-Din following the same route except that instead of it turning left if continues straight on, terminating just short of the Mausoleum.

Note that the tomb of Shagarat al-Durr stands within iron railings and is kept locked to prevent neighbourhood encroachment. To enter, permission must first be obtained from the Egyptian Antiquities Organisation, 4D Sharia Fakhry Abd al Nour, Abbassia. Tel: 839637.

The Ibn Tulun, Gayer-Anderson, Hassan, Rifa'i and the Citadel all charge a **fee** of LE1. (Your entrance ticket to the Gayer-Anderson is also valid on the same day for admission to the Islamic Museum). There may be additional fees, or at least baksheesh, for shoe coverings. You should not assume that any of these places will remain open after 4pm. An additional fee of LE5 will permit you to take photographs inside the Gayer-Anderson.

For those with limited time an **abbreviated itinerary** should include the Mosques of Ibn Tulun and Sultan Hassan.

DARB EL AHMAR

Continuing our journey northwards, let us assume we are back at the Citadel. You should leave the Citadel by the northeast entrance (the one you entered if you came up from Midan Salah al-Din), turning left as soon as you pass through the gate. Down the hill you cross over the road which issues east out of the midan and you enter Sharia el Mahga. The road plunges downhill and soon becomes Sharia Bab el Wazir, the Street of the Gate of the Vizier, and later becomes Darb el Ahmar, the Red Road, as it runs up to Bab Zuwayla. This entire district is known as **Darb el Ahmar**, a name which nowadays epitomises a poorer, broken-down section of the city. At the Citadel end which is entirely residential the street is fairly quiet and fairly filthy; it becomes livelier, and you do not notice the filth so much, as you enter the bazaar area farther north. Apart from the ruins of many old houses and some fine intact monuments, you may also encounter the gaiety of a marriage procession, a great noise of motor scooters, car horns, tambourines, ululations, whistling, chanting and cries, an amazing public racket by no more than two dozen people escorting the bride and groom through the streets.

Along Sharia Bab el Wazir
Soon after setting off down Sharia Bab el Wazir you come on your right to the **Mosque of Aqsunqur** (123), better known as the **Blue Mosque** and much beloved for the wrong reasons by tour guides. It was built in 1347 but usurped in 1652 by the Turkish Governor Ibrahim Agha who slapped up the tiles that give the mosque its popular name. The best Turkish tiles were from Iznik; these were made in Ottoman factories at Damascus and are poorly decorated and often marred as well in the glazing. They are along the qibla wall and around the walls of Agha's tomb which you enter through a door on the right side of the courtyard. The worst thing about the tiles is their inappropriateness, for the mosque is otherwise charmingly simple. A stand of palms and other trees makes the courtyard an agreeable place to linger after the hot desolate sahns of other mosques. The pillars round the courtyard, and especially the octagonal ones of the sanctuary, are crude, but contribute to the rustic pleasantness of the whole. The finest work is the carved stone minbar, which is original. On the left before entering the courtyard is the tomb of Sultan Kuchuk, The Little One, a brother of Hassan who ruled for five months at the age of six, but was then deposed, imprisoned in the Citadel, and three years later strangled by another of his brothers.

A small
strangling

54

From the street you can see behind the Aqsunqur a section of **Saladin's walls** which extended from the Fatimid city in the north to Fustat in the south, the Mamelukes using a part of its southern section to carry their aqueduct. Across the street from the mosque is a **Turkish apartment building** from 1625.

Into Darb el Ahmar

Continuing north, Sharia Bab el Wazir becomes Darb el Ahmar and set at an angle to this street, on the left-hand side, is the **Maridani Mosque** (120). Built in 1339–40 in the early Mameluke period, it is one of the oldest buildings in the quarter which until the 14th C had been Fatimid and Ayyubid cemeteries.

Entering from the hurly-burly of the street you are soon absorbed into the restfulness of the Maridani, a monument, yes, but no museum, no entry fee, no one to ask **Removing** baksheesh for shoe covers for there are none, and you **shoes** leave your shoes inside the door and walk about in your socks. Not that you need worry about form, but as a matter of interest a Muslim will carry his shoes in his left hand, sole to sole (the left hand being for unclean uses), and he will put his right foot first over the threshold. If he has not already performed the ablution outside, he will at once go to the inner fountain. Before praying, he will place his shoes on the matting, a little before the spot where his head will touch the ground, and again, to avoid contaminating the mosque, he will put his shoes one upon the other, sole to sole.

Isolation from the outside world is as much a matter of tranquil ambience as it is of ritual cleanliness. The atmosphere attracts many who come not only for prayer: here I have seen men sleeping, boys doing their homework leaning up against the qibla screen, a dozen women talking and their children playing at the fountain (the one removed from the Sultan Hassan). Yet all of these things are against the precepts of Mohammed, and even though Lane reported, 150 years ago, eating, sewing and spinning as well, these activities ceased during prayers, though here, too, I have seen the hum of irreligion continue while men were on their palms and knees, submitting themselves to Allah.

Prayers Prayers are performed five times a day, though mostly at home, with better off people rarely visiting a mosque except for Friday prayers. But wherever they are performed, prayers follow the same procedure, which is quite involved. First the worshipper will stand, facing Mecca, and inaudibly propose a prayer of so many *rek'ahs*, or inclinations of the head. He then says 'Allahu Akbar', God is great, and recites the opening chapter of the Koran, followed by three or more other verses, again says 'Allahu

Akbar' and makes an inclination of the head and body. Next he drops gently to his knees, places his palms upon the ground, his nose and forehead touching the ground between them, and during this prostration says 'I extol the perfection of my Lord, the Great', three times. Though still kneeling, he raises his head and body, again says 'God is great', and bends his head a second time to the ground and repeats what he has said before. This—and it is a simplification of the full litany—completes one rek'ah and will take about a minute, though several rek'ahs will be performed and there must be no wandering of the mind, no irregular movement and no interruptions, otherwise the procedure must be gone over from the beginning. Islam literally means submission and that is what the procedure achieves. The concentration required explains why mosques are often so austere: architecturally they should be conducive to prayer, but should not distract with decorations. That does not explain why, nowadays, and in some mosques, women should be chattering in the corner and children splashing in the fountain, yet it does all fit together most agreeably, and if you stand here in the open courtyard of the Maridani at evening, you may see a crescent moon hanging from the approving sky.

An easy rhythm of arches on slender columns runs round the courtyard, an inner and an outer series, a third and partial fourth (on either side of the mihrab) added to the qibla arcade. A wooden *screen* separates the qibla from the courtyard, a unique feature in Cairo, and, inside, the arcade is pleasantly dark. The mihrab and the minbar wall have had their mosaic decorations well restored. The dome above the mihrab is supported by two pink granite pharaonic columns. The merlons along the parapet of the courtyard are at intervals topped by curious pots. Try, if you can, to climb up the minaret for a more immediate view of the medieval city than you can get from the Citadel.

Another 150 metres up the street is the **Mosque of Qijmas al-Ishaqi** (114), built in 1480–1 during the Burgi Mameluke period. It has been squeezed into a triangular plot where a street joins Darb el Ahmar from the right, yet despite this the Mameluke fashion for rectangular illusion succeeds, at least at first glance. Inside, however, a sacrifice has been made in the cruciform plan: the north and south liwans are merely vestigal. So restricted was the space that the *kuttab*, the Koranic school usually part of the mosque, had to be sited across the street joining from the right; it is now derelict.

But the mosque itself has been very well restored and though around this period—only a few decades before the Turkish domination—Mameluke architecture began to deteriorate, there was a last bravado of decorative artistry

Fatimid keel-arches and tie-beams: Mosque of Salih Talai

with fine marble inlays and beautifully carved stone and stucco. Within this covered mosque is a feast of detail, yet all of it harmonious and restful; nothing jitters, jumps or jars. The east and west liwans are supported by arches with a slight return, the stonework in alternating red and white, the vaults very fine and the stucco windows excellent. The inlaid marble floor is covered with mats (the mosque is in daily use), but the keeper will lift these if you ask, the best section being the mosaic flooring of the east liwan. You can also ask to go up the minaret from which there is a clear view of Bab Zuwayla.

The tomb chamber by the entrance is plain and dignified beneath a lofty dome. But Qijmas, Master of the Sultan's Horse and officer in charge of the yearly pilgrimage to Mecca, died in Syria and is buried at Damascus; the chamber contains the more recent tomb of a 19th C holy man. Mamelukes and Turks of Qijmas' rank built not only for Allah or themselves, but also for the community, and a *sabil* or public watering fountain was often provided. This was in keeping with Mohammed's reply when asked what was the most meritorious act: 'To give people water to drink'. You can see its grille outside at what was a convenient height for drawing water 500 years ago, though now well below street level.

Outside the Gate of the Fatimid City
Darb el Ahmar now bends to the west, a surviving section of **Fatimid wall** concealed by the building on your right, and opens into a square dominated by **Bab Zuwayla** (see later chapter), the massive southern gate into the Fatimid city. The place has long had a reputation for being unlucky, perhaps because it led out to the cemeteries now built over by the Darb el Ahmar quarter, though also it was the site of **Public** public executions. Tumanbay, the last independent **executions** Mameluke sultan, was hanged here by the Turks. Twice the rope broke, the third time his neck.

The street running directly south from Bab Zuwayla is the continuation of the principal Fatimid street to the north and extends all the way down, past the Mosque of Ibn Tulun and through Saladin's walls to the vicinity of the Mausoleum of Imam al-Shaf'i. This was the longest thoroughfare of the medieval city and along here amidst great festivity the Mecca pilgrims would begin their arduous journey. It changes its name several times and can be worth following for its own sake a little to the south where it is first the Street of the Tentmakers, becoming less colourful as the Street of the Saddlemakers before crossing Sharia el Qalaa.

On the corner of this street and Darb el Ahmar, facing the square, is the **Mosque of Salih Talai** (116), built in 1160

Classic Fatimid mosque towards the close of the Fatimid period. A congregational mosque, perfectly rectangular in the Fatimid pattern, it is one of the most handsome in Cairo. A lower level of shops, again once at street level, was part of Salih Talai's *waqf* or endowment, as other mosques might have had fields or adjacent apartment buildings, the rents contributing to the mosque's upkeep. The facade, therefore, would have been higher, its effect still more imposing. Its five keel-arches, supported by classical columns linked by wooden tie-beams, are flanked by sunken false arches or panels topped by stylised shell niches — the whole a perfect expression of the Fatimid style. The arches, however, form a *narthex* or porch unique in Cairo. Along its interior wall another set of panels, each one immediately behind an open keel-arch, runs in muted harmony. In its proportion and reserve the narthex is a fine composition in classical measure. The mosque interior is spacious, an agreeable rhythm of keel-arches and tie-beams running around the arcades.

PRACTICAL INFORMATION

To reach the starting point of this tour go to the Midan Salah al-Din (see the *Practical Information* section at the end of the previous chapter).

The mosques visited in this chapter are still very much places of worship rather than tourist sights and they are usually open throughout the day and into the evening. Nevertheless, tourists will often have to pay an entrance **fee** of LE1, and baksheesh should be paid for services, eg shoe coverings, being taken up a minaret.

The pleasure of this itinerary is the slow walk and the occasional pause at the mosques along the way — enjoyment of atmosphere. The person in a hurry might therefore wish to skip this chapter altogether, though the best advice is that he should not be in a hurry. An **abbreviated itinerary** should bring you to the square before the Mosque of Salih Talai and Bab Zuwayla; this could be combined with a visit to the Islamic Museum or with the walk from Bab Zuwayla to Khan el Khalili (see following chapters).

THE ISLAMIC MUSEUM

The Islamic Museum, to the west of the Bab Zuwayla, is at the intersection of Sharias el Qalaa and Port Said, its entrance on the latter through a garden to which you should return later. Of course the museum could be visited before you explore any part of Islamic Cairo, but for the neophyte, anyway, a visit at this point, halfway through the tour, might be best: you will already have seen enough to make you conversant with form and curious about detail, and you will explore the Fatimid city with greater appreciation.

A revelation, met especially here, is how much you miss human and animal representation in Islamic art and architecture. This is a museum without statues or paintings, where nearly every object is beautifully worked design. A different sort of attention is required, and perhaps you wish sometimes, more here than at other museums, that the exhibits could have remained *in situ*, admired as parts **Preservation of** of a whole. But then the collection began, in 1880, precisely **Cairo's Islamic** because the monuments from which they mostly came had **treasures** suffered a long period of neglect — it was only then, in part at European instigation, that the Egyptian government first seriously undertook preservation of Cairo's Islamic treasures.

The exhibits are well presented and lit and are arranged in 23 rooms which proceed chronologically for the most part, though some rooms specialise in examples of a single subject, eg textiles, from several periods. Though no guide book is available, the exhibits are numbered and labelled, often in English and French as well as in Arabic. A satisfying tour can be accomplished in an hour and a half. With one exception, all the rooms are on one floor. A brief outline follows, but note that some rooms may be closed and their contents either inaccessible or to be found in another nearby room.

Note that because the entrance used to be along the side of the building facing Sharia Port Said, the room numbers start from there; but because you now enter through the north garden (reached also from Sharia Port Said) you find yourself first in Room 7 and so should walk straight through rooms 7, 10, 4B and 2 in order to begin at Room 1.

A Tour of the Museum

Room 1 contains **recent acquisitions**, though also some permanent exhibits, including a magnificent lantern, 14th C, of bronze chased with silver from the Sultan Hassan mosque.

Room 2 deals with the **Ummayad** period (7th–8th C) whose art was representational and drew on Hellenistic and Sassanian (Persian) sources.

Room 3 is **Abbasid** (8th–10th C) and includes **Tulunid** (9th–10th C) works. Here there is greater stylisation, with the emphasis on decoration rather than representation, with great use of stucco, characterised by its slant cut. There are stucco panels from Samarra in Iraq, and tombstones, of which 3904, dating from 858, has fine Kufic inscriptions.

Room 4 displays works of the **Fatimid** period (10th–12th C) with examples of very fine woodwork, carved with human and animal figures and foliage. The Fatimids, who were Shi'ites, did not observe the Sunni prohibition on representation of high living forms, and were much influenced by the Persians, whose craftsmen they imported.

Room 4B, off Room 4, has fine wood, marble and stucco carving of the **Ayyubid** period (12th–13th C).

Before entering *Room 5*, note above the dividing arch the windows of openwork plaster filled with coloured glass (16th–18th C, Ottoman period). (The museum, incidentally, is not visited nearly as much as it deserves to be, so that you often receive personal attention. In this case, the attendant will turn off the main lights and illuminate the coloured windows for effect.) The room contains works of the **Mameluke** period (13th–16th C). There is a beautiful 14th C fountain sunk into the floor (the attendant will turn it on). Despite the bloody succession of Mameluke sultans, Egypt during much of this period enjoyed peace and the decorative arts flourished. A Chinese influence was felt in Mameluke ceramics and pottery. Soft woods were inlaid with ivory, bone, tin and ebony, usually in star-polygons, the Naskhi cursive supplanted the squat Kufic style of decorative inscription, and arabesque floral designs found favour. A 13th C wooden door (602) at the far end of the room shows both square Kufic and cursive Naskhi calligraphy. It is from the Mausoleum of al-Salih Ayyub.

Rooms 6–10 are devoted to **woodwork**, illustrating the development of the art. In *Room 6* on the far wall is a carved frieze originally from the western Fatimid palace, ie 10th C, showing scenes of hunting, music and other courtly activities rarely found in Islamic art. In *Room 7* are *mashrabiyyas*, wooden screens which preserved the privacy of the house from the gaze of the street while still admitting refreshing breezes. They were also used to screen off interior harem rooms from courtyards and reception halls. The projecting niches were for placing porous water jars for cooling. *Room 8* has examples of inlaid wood, while *Room 9* displays wood and bronze work.

In *Room 10*, off Room 9, you will be asked to sit down on a lattice-backed seat round a column fountain which will be turned on for you and illuminated. This is a restful and eye-filling place to linger: gaze up at the exquisite woodwork ceiling, carved and coffered, with three dome recesses, the centre one with windows round it for ladies of the harem to see below. The period is 17th–18th C.

Room 11 is hung with 14th C bronze chandeliers, and in the cases are various **metalwork** objects, eg a perfume brazier (15111, Case 7).

Room 12 contains armour and weapons, many of them chased and inlaid. In Case 7 are swords belonging to Mehmet II, who conquered Constantinople (4264), and Suleyman the Magnificent (4263). And another in the same case, opposite the windows on the right, which has had a remarkable history: the sword of Muradbey, commander of the Mamelukes, was taken by the French general Murat after he had chased the Mamelukes up the Nile, and was presented to Napoleon who in turn wore it when calling on the Directory shortly before seizing power on 18 Brumaire 1799. He had it with him also at Waterloo, and leaving it in his carriage which he abandoned in haste after the battle, it was presented to Wellington.

Rooms 13–16 contain **pottery** of various periods from Egypt and as far west as Spain, as far east as China.

Room 17 is up the stairs on your right as you enter from the garden. It displays textiles and carpets of various periods from Egypt and elsewhere in the Islamic world.

Leading off Room 19 is an outdoor court which is *Room 18* and is principally of Turkish headstones and tombs, but also other **stonework** objects, including a sundial and water level measures.

Room 19 is devoted to the art of the book with many illuminated **manuscripts**, mostly Korans. This may be a sign of these increasingly fundamentalist times. Until recently, pride of place was given to manuscripts of Avicenna on anatomy and botany, but these have been removed. He lived from 980 to 1037 and was one of the greatest physicians of the Middle Ages. Chaucer mentions him in *The Canterbury Tales*. He was an example of the way in which the Arabs passed on the medical theory of the Greeks, enriching it by practical observation and clinical experience. This room now illuminates merely the eclipse of their genius.

Room 20 exhibits **Turkish** art since the 15th C including tapestries, china and jewellery.

Between Rooms 20 and 21 are enamelled glass **lamps** which the attendant will illuminate, while there are more glass lamps in cases round the walls of *Room 21* and in the centre a fine Isfahan carpet that once belonged to King Farouk. The lamps are from mosques (and include some of those now entirely missing from the liwans of the Sultan Hassan) and are arranged chronologically from left to right from the 12th through the 15th C.

Room 22 contains **Persian** objects, mostly pottery, some of which (Cases 1 and 2) have been copied from Chinese models.

Room 23 is for **temporary exhibitions**.

The garden can now be enjoyed on your way out; there are welcome refreshments for sale in a flower-planted setting with a shaded gazebo, a fountain, columns and other large stone pieces. Particularly fine are the large marble panels bearing Fatimid figurative reliefs of plants, birds, fish and animals.

Story of the fountain Concerning the fountain, there is a story that I have from a member of the Monasterly family to whom it once belonged. The fountain was in their palace on Roda. Its purpose was to run a stream of water through channels decorated with creatures of the Nile, the channels encircling a large dining table, the flowing water keeping the diners cool. The palace was sequestrated by King Farouk, but when Queen Marie of Roumania announced her intention to pay the family a visit Farouk kindly let them have the use of the palace for one last dinner. By now, however, the fountain would not work; yet the water flowed, the guests were cooled—the old servants were brought back, my friend explained, and formed a human chain between the Nile and the back of the fountain into which they tipped bucket after bucket of water throughout the dinner. 'They so enjoyed it', my friend said of the servants, 'wasn't that *sweet*?' The Monasterly Palace is now the Centre for Art and Life.

In the same building but on the upper floor is the **Egyptian Library** with its entrance on Sharia el Qalaa. Containing over 750,000 volumes and a vast collection of manuscripts of the Koran dating back to the 8th C and, most outstanding visually, a collection of Persian manuscripts adorned with miniatures of imaginative conception and frequently employing living forms as distinct from the purely ornamental art of the Korans.

PRACTICAL INFORMATION

The Islamic Museum is at Midan Ahmed Maher, where Sharia Port Said and Sharia el Qalaa intersect. A **taxi** can take you here or to nearby Bab Zuwayla (the driver may know it better as Bab al-Mitwalli), or you can take the **No. 66 bus** from Midan el Tahrir.

The museum is open daily from 9am to 4pm except Fridays when it is closed from 11am to 1.30pm. There is an entrance **fee** of LE2 (LE1 for students with card) which is also valid on the same day for the Gayer-Anderson House.

Provided you do not use a flash, you may take unlimited photographs for LE5. With a flash, the fee is LE5 *per photo*.

BAB ZUWAYLA TO KHAN EL KHALILI

Entering the Fatimid city

We now turn to **Bab Zuwayla**, built at the same time (11th C) and in a plan similar to Bab al-Futuh and Bab al-Nasr to the north. These three are the last surviving of the 60 gates that once encircled medieval Cairo and which, well into the 19th C, were shut at night, enclosing the city's then 240,000 population. Except that Bab Zuwayla had long since found itself outflanked by the growth of the city to the south (where it was delimited by Saladin's walls), and in fact marked the city centre. The architects of all three were Armenians from Edessa, and the projecting round towers connected by a walkway and an arch repeating the curve of the gateway below show Byzantine rather than Arab inspiration. Springing from the massive towers are the elegant minarets of the Mosque of Muayyad, its serrated dome farther back seeming to rise between them.

The gate was named for the al-Zawila, a Berber tribe whose Fatimid soldiery were quartered nearby. But most inhabitants know it as the al-Mitwalli after El Kutb al-Mitwalli, the holiest man alive at any one time, who would assume a humble demeanour and simple dress, and station himself inconspicuously, even invisibly, at certain favourite places. Bab Zuwayla was the most famous of these in Egypt, though he could flit to Tanta in the Delta, or to Mecca and back, in an instant. His service was to reprove the impious, expose the sanctimonious, and to distribute evils and blessings, the awards of destiny. Into the earlier part of this century, passersby would recite the opening of the Koran, while those with headache would drive a nail into the door, or sufferers from a recent toothache would fix their tooth to it as a charm against recurrence. Locks of hair, bits of clothing, would also be attached by the sick in search of a miracle — indeed they still are; and, it is said, the saint still makes his presence known by a gleam of light mysteriously appearing behind the west door.

Climbing the minarets above Bab Zuwayla

Passing through the gate, you should enter the **Mosque of Muayyad** (190) on your left, less for any intrinsic interest, though it is restful and has a garden, than for access to the top of Bab Zuwayla or even up one of the minarets. This is a view of medieval Cairo from its heart and it is splendid. The last of the great open courtyard congregational mosques, the Muayyad was built in 1416–20 by the Burgi Mameluke Muayyad Shaykh who had been imprisoned on the spot before becoming sultan.

Souks and Okels

This street running north from Bab Zuwayla is Sharia Muizz (named for the caliph of the Fatimid conquest), though over

Prayers before emerging from the Mosque of Muayyad

its distance between Bab Zuwayla and Bab al-Futuh it enjoys successive traditional names, each one demarcating a souk reserved to a particular trade or the sale of a particular type of merchandise—ensuring, subject to proper bargaining, price control by competition between neighbours. Alongside Muayyad's mosque, for example, the street is Shari'es-Sukkariya, the sugar bazaar. Competition, however, was not the only control on market prices: the Mohtesib, an officer on horseback, would regularly ride through the souks, preceded by a man carrying a pair of scales and followed by the executioner. If spot checks revealed short weights, a butcher, for example, or a baker would have his nose pierced with a hook, a piece of meat, a loaf of bread, suspended from it as the poor man was himself tied to the grilled window of a mosque and left to endure the heat of the sun, the indifference of passersby. One butcher who sold short was deprived of that much flesh from his own body, while a seller of *kunefeh*, a sweet-meat made from that vermicelli pasta (*atayif*) you still see prepared along the streets at night, was fried on his own copper tray for overcharging.

Continuing up to the intersection with the modern Sharia al-Azhar, you find yourself between two Mameluke buildings, the **Madrasa of Sultan al-Ghuri** (189) on the left and his **Mausoleum** (67) on the right. Al-Ghuri was the penultimate Mameluke sultan and the last to reign for any duration (1500–16). A keen polo player into his seventies, a grandiose builder, an arbitrary despot, a torturer, murderer and thief, in short no less than what you would expect a Mameluke sultan to be, he inaugurated his madrasa in May 1503 with a great banquet attended by the Abbasid caliph and all the principal civil, military and religious officials, the souks down to Bab Zuwayla magnificently illuminated and decorated. But though agreeably exotic at first impression, with strong lines and bold *ablaq* (that red and white pattern of the minaret with its curious topping of five small bulbous domes) on closer inspection there is lack of elegance in the details, and in climbing up to the roof you see that the ablaq is not contrasting stone but crudely painted on.

Mameluke sunset   Across the street, the mausoleum dome, now collapsed, had to be rebuilt three times during al-Ghuri's reign, and as though shrewdly realising that this might be an unsafe place to be buried, he got himself killed outside Aleppo in a losing battle against the Turks. His luckless successor, that same Tumanbay who was hanged three times at Bab Zuwayla, is buried here instead.

Heading east along Sharia al-Azhar you come after about 100 metres to the **Okel of al-Ghuri** (64) on your right, unmistakably Mameluke with its ablaq masonry and strong, square lines. Built in 1504–5, this is Cairo's best preserved example of a merchants' hotel, the animals quartered on the ground floor and their masters above. The courtyard would be the scene of unloading aromatic cargoes, with buyers and sellers sitting round and bargaining. This okel was built just at the time that the Portuguese were dealing a blow to Egypt's overland trade with the East by their discovery of new routes round the Cape to India. Even so, as late as 1835 there were still 200 okels serving Cairo's bazaars.

The Religious Heart of Islamic Cairo

The famous **Mosque of al-Azhar** (97), 'the most blooming', is 100 metres east of al-Ghuri's caravanserai, the first mosque of the Fatimid city (completed in 971), the oldest university in the world and the foremost centre of Islamic theology. Its age and importance have caused it to be rebuilt and added to many times, the result confusing and unremarkable. The court and arcades are basically Fatimid, but their interest lies in the people gathered here, students and teachers at lessons, some pacing back and forth, mumbling to themselves, memorising religious texts, others dozing.

Throughout the millenium of its existence, al-Azhar has offered free instruction and board to students from all over the Islamic world, from West Africa to the East Indies, its courses sometimes lasting 15 years. *Riwaqs* or apartments are set aside around three sides of the court for specific nationalities or provinces of Egypt, and here students have tradition-

66

ally studied religious, moral, civil and criminal law, grammar, rhetoric, theology, logic, algebra and calculations on the Muslim calendar which is based on the moon, its festivals changeable but always advancing against the secular solar calendar. The Chapel of the Blind at the eastern angle of al-Azhar accommodates blind students, once notorious for their outrageous behaviour. Fanatical in their belief and easily thinking themselves persecuted, they would rush out into the streets, snatching at turbans, beating people with their staves and groping about for infidels to kill.

Oldest university in the world

Al-Azhar's religious curriculum has remained unchanged since the days of Saladin, who turned al-Azhar from a hotbed of Shi'ism to the home of orthodoxy, though Nasser obliged the university to include, too, schools of medicine, science and foreign languages, so that now in many ways it is competitive with other institutions of higher education in Egypt. The modern university buildings are behind the mosque proper.

You enter the mosque through the double-arched Gate of the Barbers (the only one open to visitors) where formerly students had their heads shaved, and for a bit of baksheesh can ascend the *minaret of Qaytbay*. Passing into the courtyard, on the left is the *library*, worth a visit, and to the right a 14th C *madrasa* with a fine mihrab. The *sanctuary hall* directly opposite the entry gate is very deep, though in Fatimid times it did not extend beyond the fifth row of columns (that is five rows beyond the two of the east arcade), and the original mihrab remains. These columns were taken mostly from early churches. The sanctuary was extended to eight rows in the 18th C and a new mihrab placed at its farthest, qibla, wall.

Leaving al-Azhar and walking north, you pass under the busy Sharia al-Azhar and stand before the **Mosque of Sayyidna al-Hussein**, a modern structure with slender Turkish-style minarets built on a Fatimid site. This is the main congregational mosque of Cairo and the President of the Republic comes here on feast days for prayers, while the open square before it is the centre for popular nightly celebrations throughout the month of Ramadan — well worth seeing.

The Hussein, named for a grandson of the Prophet, is supposedly forbidden to non-Muslims, though I have several times been invited inside. Hussein's head, brought to Cairo in 1153 in a green silk bag, is in the mausoleum (it is also said to be in the Great Mosque in Damascus), a relic of one of the most critical events in Islamic history, the schism between the Sunni majority and the Shi'ites.

The Sunni-Shi'ite schism

Mohammed was more than a prophet, he organised the Arab tribes into an enduring political and military force that within a hundred years or so of his death in 632 advanced as

67

far west as Morocco and Spain, as far north as Poitiers and as far east as the Indus. But Mohammed died without naming a successor. His son-in-law Ali, husband of the Prophet's daughter Fatima, advanced his claim but after some argument Abu Bakr, one of Mohammed's companions, won acceptance as *Khalifat rasul-Allah* or Successor to the Apostle of God. Abu Bakr was succeeded by Omar who was succeded on his death by Othman, an old, weak and vacillating man, but a member of the powerful Umayyad family of Mecca. Tribal tensions within the ever-expanding Arab empire led to revolt and his murder in 656. Again Ali put himself forward as the natural inheritor of the caliphate, for not only was he related to Mohammed through Fatima, but he was a man of considerable religious learning and sincerity, while his supporters claimed the Umayyads were no more than power-seeking opportunists. To some extent both sides cloaked political and economic aspirations in religious arguments. Ali however was opposed by Aisha, who had been Mohammed's favourite wife, along with her Umayyad family and many of Mohammed's surviving companions. He took to arms and won his first battle, but later saw his authority dissolve when rebels advanced on his army with copies of the Koran fixed to the points of their spears and his troops refused to fight. Ali was assassinated and the Umayyads were installed once again in the caliphate.

The real wound to Islam occurred, however, when Ali's son — no mere in-law of the Prophet but of his blood — led a revolt against the by now overwhelming forces of the Umayyads and after a fanatical struggle was slain with all his men. In a sense the Prophet's own blood had been shed — excusable, said the Ummayads, for Hussein was no more than an outlaw; martyrdom, replied those who had supported Ali and Hussein. It was on this matter of succession — divine right versus might — that Islam was riven, for the partisans or *Shia* of Ali refused to accept as caliph any but Ali's descendants, while the *Sunni*, followers of the *sunnia*, The Way, barred the caliphate to the Prophet's descendants for all time.

In fact, the Shi'ites went on to win some notable victories as when the Fatimids took Egypt, and to this day one-tenth of all Muslims (Iranians, most Iraqis and significant numbers in Yemen, Syria, Lebanon and eastern Arabia) still hold to the Shi'ite conviction that with the deaths of Ali and Hussein the greater part of Islam was stained with betrayal. All the same, this division within Islam is much less important than the doctrinal rifts within Christianity, and it is remarkable that it is here in the old Fatimid city, by the mausoleum supposedly containing the very head of the Shi'ite martyr, that the president of thoroughly Sunni Egypt should come to pray.

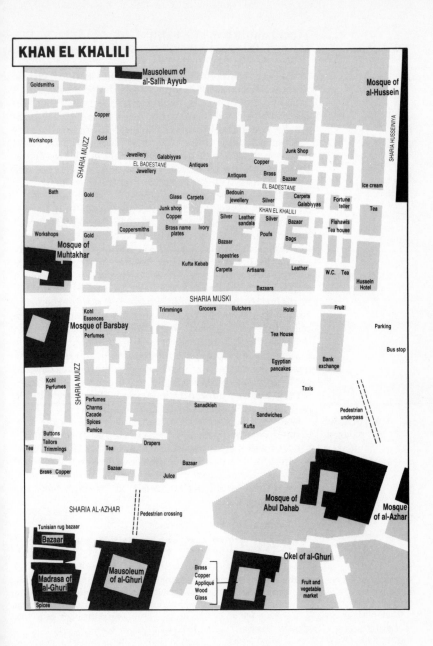

KHAN EL KHALILI

Muski and Khan el Khalili

The bazaars

Muski and Khan el Khalili are used interchangeably by both foreigners and Egyptians alike to describe what are historically two different bazaars. **Muski** lies astride Sharia el Muski, a street of Mohammed Ali's period running east from Midan Ataba, pots, pans, plastic bowls and other prosaic wares sold at its western end but blending with the Oriental atmosphere of Khan el Khalili which it joins to the east.

Khan el Khalili is the larger and older of the two, and grew round a khan or caravanserai built in 1382 by Sultan Barquq's Master of Horse, Garkas el Khalili. It became known as the Turkish bazaar during the Ottoman period and has always attracted foreign merchants — Jews, Armenians, Persians and non-Egyptian Arabs — and so it is not surprising that today, along with the Muski, it is Cairo's tourist bazaar, selling souvenirs, perfume oils, jewellery, leather goods and fabrics. Of course the sight of so many tourists invites relentless importuning, but there is adventure all the same. Escape down back alleyways where an artisan sitting in his hole in the wall may patiently be making beads one by one from rough bits of stone, turning them on a spindle by means of a bow. Or start in bargaining and then break off — an accepted, indeed the expert pattern — and instead sip a proffered glass of tea, idling for hours if you like upon a pile of carpets without there being any sense of the need for business. Or go into Fishawi's, the famous café just off Midan Sayyidna Hussein. Here you can have the chance of easy conversation and a gentle smoke of a water pipe ('Do not inhale, it is not hashish.').

The Fatimid palaces

Khan el Khalili extends in part over the site of the now vanished Fatimid palaces which covered an area of 400,000 square metres and housed 12,000 domestics. The palaces, al-Muizz on the east side of Sharia Muizz and al-Aziz on the west, loomed like mountains when seen from afar; near to, they could not be seen at all, so high were the surrounding walls.

PRACTICAL INFORMATION

Instructions for reaching the start of this itinerary are the same as for the Islamic Museum.

Remember that there is often a **fee** of LE1 at mosques, etc, classed as Islamic monuments. Also you will need small change for services performed.

The Okel (or Wakala) of al-Ghuri serves also as a permanent exhibition of fellahin and Bedouin folk crafts, and those of Nubia and the oases. Folk music and dancing troupes sometimes perform in the courtyard. Open from 9am to 5pm daily (9–11am, 2–4pm during Ramadan). **Fee** LE2.

An **abbreviated itinerary** should at least involve a stroll from Bab Zuwayla to Khan el Khalil for the passing flavour. This could be combined with a visit to the Islamic Museum.

TO THE NORTHERN WALLS

Street of the Coppersmiths

Sharia Muizz, as you leave the awning-covered alleyways of Khan el Khalili and walk north along it, is the Street of the Coppersmiths, some bashing of metal, much flashing of sunlight. Some reminders of the Fatimid period survive, though mostly the monuments are Mameluke. There should be a mosque on every street, it is said. Here mosques fight for every corner, their domes and minarets bunched like palms in an oasis grove. The scene is still that of the *Thousand and One Nights*, ostensibly set in Baghdad, though Baghdad by then had been razed by Tamerlane and it was the Cairo of the Mamelukes that was described. Sweet juices, cool water is sold in the street, the waterseller with a large flask slung under one arm like a bagpipe, round his waist the cups. He leans forward to pour, and for a moment you imagine this an obeisance to a passing sultan, and in the sweep of robes, the clattering of donkey carts, the bursts of reflected light from the coppersmiths' stalls, you easily imagine a triumphal entry, a parade of state, singers and poets preceding the royal appearance, celebrating the achievements of his reign. You see fluttering banners of silk and gold thread, then carried before the sultan himself the jewelled saddlecloth, symbol of his sovereignty, and above his head a parasol of yellow silk surmounted with a golden cupola on which perches a golden bird, this held aloft by a prince of the blood, a band of flutes, of kettledrums, trumpets and hautboys passing now, their music mingling in the calmour of the street and then lost.

There is spectacle enough in Sharia Muizz, and behind its facades, to remind you that this was a city of beauty and mystery. Ruthless for power, cunning in government, brutal and barbarous often, the Mamelukes at their best were resourceful and vital, with an incomparable flair for architecture. Their grandiose designs, bold, vigorous and voluminous, were gracefully decorated with the play of arabesques, the embroidery of light through stained-glass windows.

The Story of Shagarat al-Durr

You come first, on the right, to the Mausoleum and Madrasa of al-Salih Ayyub, diagonally opposite the Maristan of Qalaun. Where the street now presses its way was once, in Fatimid times, a broad avenue, so broad it served as a parade ground, the great palaces looking down upon it from either side. Throughout the Fatimid and Mameluke periods, this was the very centre of Cairo.

The **Mausoleum and Madrasa of al-Salih Ayyub** (38) need to be searched for. You turn right off Muizz into a lane—there is a tiny teashop on the corner with some round brass tables outside (an agreable place to sit for a while). A short distance along the lane is an arch set into a facade with a Fatimid-style minaret rising from it. This is the madrasa, and you enter what remains of it by turning left into what is now used by neighbourhood youths as a playing field, liwans to east and west. The mausoleum is reached by returning to the Street of the Coppersmiths and turning right. You will see the dome on your right, and the door will be locked, but ask (or gesture to) anyone nearby for the key: they will find the keeper.

The interest of this place is historical, for it marks a political and architectural transition. Al-Salih Ayyub was the last ruler of Saladin's dynasty. His wife, who completed his madrasa and mausoleum after he died in 1249, was Shagarat al-Durr, a beautiful Armenian or Turkish slave girl who ushered in Mameluke rule. While it has Fatimid elements, the madrasa was also the first to provide for all four schools of Sunni Islam, and was the first also to link madrasa and mausoleum—in short, it was the prototype for the Mameluke mosque-madrasa-mausolea to follow. Throughout the Mameluke period it was used as Cairo's central court (the schools teaching, amongst other things, law as at al-Azhar), and the street outside, Sharia Muizz, served as the place of execution.

Tree of Pearls Shagarat al-Durr, whose name means Tree of Pearls, shares with Hatshepsut and Cleopatra that rare distinction of having been a female ruler of Egypt. She rose to power at a critical moment, when St Louis at the head of the Sixth Crusade seized Damietta in the Delta. Ayyub, dying from cancer, was too weak to dislodge him, and St Louis was content to await the sultan's death and what he imagined would be the collapse of government and all resistance to Christian occupation of the country.

But Shagarat al-Durr was of independent nomadic stock, a society in which women went unveiled and were the equals of their men. She hid her husband's corpse in the Mameluke barracks on Roda while pretending he was merely ailing, and for three months ruled Egypt by appearing to transmit orders from Ayyub to his generals.

Egypt played for time and offered the Crusaders Jerusalem if they would abandon Damietta. St Louis refused. But meanwhile in the heat, and fed bad fish by the Delta people, the Crusaders became sick with scurvy and plague. St Louis then accepted the offer of Jerusalem, but it was the Egyptians now who refused, and the Mameluke **The capture of** general Baybars fell upon the Crusaders, capturing St **St Louis** Louis, who had to buy his freedom with a vast indemnity and the renunciation of all claim to Egypt.

Shagarat al-Durr now openly proclaimed herself sultana

and for 80 days was the only female Muslim ruler in Middle Eastern history, but the Abbasid Caliph refused to recognise her, quoting the Prophet who had said, 'The people that make a woman their ruler are past saving'. So she married the leader of her Mameluke slave-warriors, Aybak, ruling through him, but when she heard he was considering another marriage she hired assassins to murder him in his bath. Hearing his screams, seeing his body hacked at with swords, at the last moment she tried to save his life, but the assassins went on: 'If we stop halfway through, he will kill both you and us'.

When the murder was discovered, Shagarat al-Durr offered to marry the new Mameluke chief, but she was imprisoned instead and is said to have spent her last days grinding up all her jewels so that no other woman should wear them. The Mamelukes had discovered their power to make and unmake rulers; in future they ruled themselves. Shagarat al-Durr was turned over to the wife she had made Aybak divorce who instructed her female slaves to beat her to death with bath clogs. They tossed her naked body over the Citadel wall to be devoured by dogs. Her few remains were deposited in her tomb on the edge of the Southern Cemetery not too far from the Mosque of Ibn Tulun.

Qalaun, al-Nasr and Barquq

A splendour of domes and minarets

Looking up and across Sharia Muizz you see on its west side the splendid cluster of domes and minarets that are the Madrasa and Mausoleum of Qalaun, the Mausoleum of al-Nasr, his son and successor, and the Mosque of Barquq. Qalaun—the name means duck and has an absurd ring in Arabic—was one of the ablest, most successful and long-lived (1220–90) of the notoriously short-lived Mameluke sultans, who moreover founded a dynasty lasting nearly 100 years. His name suggests Mongol origins, and he is known to have been brought from the lower Volga region, ruled at the time by the Golden Horde. It was al-Salih Ayyub, buried across the street, who first began importing slaves from there, employing them as bodyguards. Qalaun served the country of his purchase well: Damascus and Baghdad had fallen to the Mongols, Egypt and Arabia the sole remaining bulwarks of Islam; Baybars checked the threat, Qalaun eliminated it, and then marched against the Crusaders at Acre, their last stonghold in the Holy Land, but died enroute. An outstanding builder, his tribute to his Christian enemies was the adoption of Romanesque elements in his complex here, the **Maristan, Madrasa and Mausoleum of Qalaun** (43).

First you go through the gate and down a wide tree-shaded walk, the heat and noise of the Street of the Coppersmiths falling away behind you. At the end is a modern hospital, built within the vaster limits of Qalaun's **maristan** or hospital and insane asylum — a hospital has stood on this spot for 700 years. Three great liwans of the original remain, the windows of the east liwan still displaying their carved stucco surrounds. The north liwan, it seems, is now used as a dump for surgical dressings.

Islamic enlightenment Islam was a wonder of enlightened medical care at a time when the ill, especially the mad, were pariahs in Christian Europe. From Spain to Persia, hospitals flourished, were divided into clinics, surgery was perfected, such delicate operations as the removal of cataracts were performed, musicians and singers entertained the sick, and upon their discharge patients were given sums of money to enable them to live until they could again find employment.

Returning now to the street and turning left, the wall on your left-hand side is that of Qalaun's **madrasa**. At the far corner the line of the building then retreats and you come to what was the original entrance to the maristan. The entrance opens onto a corridor, blocked at the far end, which runs between the mausoleum on the right and the madrasa on the left. During recent reconstruction of the madrasa the opportunity was taken to excavate for clues to the Fatimids' western palace which stood here. The plan is a courtyard with a liwan at either end, the sanctuary or eastern liwan suggesting a north Syrian basilical church, with three aisles and classical columns. The stucco work farther in from the arch is original.

Qalaun's **mausoleum** is off the other side of the corridor. The plan has been influenced by the Dome of the Rock at Jerusalem, well known to the sultan: an octagon approaching the circular within a square, the arches supported by square piers and classical columns. The dome has been restored. The structure perhaps does not seem light enough, the decorations too rich, and the mashrabiyya screen obstructs a total view (the best is from the entrance) — though it also has the effect of making the relatively small interior seem endless. But there is splendour all the same, in carved stucco, the stone inlay, the wood ornamentation, slowly revealed as your eyes get used to the filtered coloured light from the stained-glass windows — those high, double round-arched windows with oculi above, framed (from both inside and out on the street) by deeply recessed pointed arches, Qalaun's borrowing of the Romanesque.

On your way out through the corridor, have a look at its beamed and coffered ceiling, which is marvellous. The street is just before you, yet in this complex all has been private, cool and quiet, birds chirping, trees and shade and shafts of sunlight. The buildings and their purpose reveal a dignity and humanity; they provide the peace by which you recognise an unexpected civilisation.

The next building along, that is continuing north on Sharia Muizz and on the left, is the **Mausoleum of al-Nasr Mohammed** (44), now ruinous except for the facade with its Gothic doorway, removed from the Crusader Church of St John when al-Nasr completed his father's work and took Acre. Al-Nasr's reign marked the zenith of Mameluke civilistion; his principal monuments are the mosque on the Citadel and the aqueduct bringing water there from the Nile. He is in fact buried next door in Qalaun's mausoleum.

The third of this group is the **Mosque of Barquq** (187), the first Burgi Mameluke sultan. It dates from 1386, about a century later than Qalaun's buildings, and the change in style is evident; the minaret, for example, is octagonal and, compared to the square blocks of Qalaun's, slender, while here is the high monumental entrance topped with stalactite decorations, seen also at the Sultan Hassan, which became typical of Mameluke architecture. This mosque-madrasa, in cruciform plan, was in use until this century and has been well maintained and restored. This portal is of black and white marble, the doors of bronze inlaid with silver. The sanctuary liwan is flat-ceilinged, not vaulted like the others, and receives support from four pharaonic columns of porphyry quarried in the Eastern Desert. The exquisite domed tomb chamber with marbled floors and walls of varying colours, painted ceiling, latticed and stained-glass windows and ornate wooden stalactites in the corners, contains the grave of one of Barquq's daughters — he was removed to his mausoleum in the Northern Cemetery.

Some Grand Cairene Houses Along the Way

Nearby are two houses of the Bahri Mameluke period. The **House of Uthman Katkhuda** (50) is in the street running east from Sharia Muizz, opposite Qalaun's mausoleum. It is about halfway down on the left-hand side. The doorway is entirely ordinary, but knock, or go to the apartment up the stairs, and someone will appear to show you round. (When soliciting local assistance, baksheesh is expected — usually demanded; but you should avoid paying until you have seen everything you want to, otherwise the demand for baksheesh will be made again and again, at each stage.)

Katkhuda was an 18th C lieutenant governor of the city who made what in fact was a mid-14th C palace into his home. Only a part of the whole remains, but it is an impressive example of Mameluke domestic architecture. Suddenly you are in a narrow hall of enormous height, its bare stone walls rising to the support of a wooden dome, distant sunlight streaming through the windows of its octagonal drum. This was the reception room, and guests sat in the raised area at the south end. The walls were once wainscotted with marble; the woodwork remains, though the consoles within the arches date from the 16th C. Ask to go up to the roof for a view of the quarter, and look at the *malqaf* or ventilator, a rectangular scoop common to old Cairene houses and always facing north to catch the Mediterranean breeze. One of the best things about this place is that you will almost certainly be the only visitor, and its fresh bareness invites pleasing, undisturbed thoughts of moving in and where to put the furniture.

Traditional air conditioning

The other house, even more so a palace, is the **Qasr Beshtak** (34). This is back on Sharia Muizz, just to the north of Barquq's mosque and on the right-hand side. The entrance is the second door along the little street of the north facade — and again you will have to find someone, with some difficulty this time, who has the key.

The Emir Beshtak was married to the daughter of al-Nasr and was a man of great wealth. He built his palace on part of the foundations of the eastern Fatimid palace and it once rose to five storeys, with running water on all floors. You pass though a courtyard, up some stairs, and enter the harem reception room, vaster yet than Katkhuda's with mashrabiyya screens along the galleries. From these there is a perfectly medieval view of the streets below.

Koranic school and fountain

The **Sabil Kuttab of Abdul Katkhuda** (21) was built in 1744 by Uthman Katkhuda's son and is one of the most charming structures in Cairo. It stands on a triangular plot, causing a fork in the street, the kuttab's porches overhanging the roadways on either side, the great grille of what was the fountain at its base facing south towards you as you approach. The kutab is still used as the neighbourhood Koranic school, while the rest of the block is taken up with a renovated 14th C apartment building.

You continue along the left-hand fork and at last, on the next block, on the right-hand side, discover a rare surviving Fatimid structure in this Mameluke-dominated part of the city. The **Mosque of al-Aqmar** (33) dates from 1125 and displays a typically Fatimid keel-arch portal. The niche ribbing, used here for the first time, was to become a favourite Cairene motif. The medallion set into the niche ribbing is very finely executed. The recesses on either side of the portal have stalactite decorations, also appearing here for the first time and later taken up by the Mamelukes. The interior is original, but the slapdash minaret is modern. Aqmar means moonlit, so named for the pale stone — the Fatimids, who meant to stay, building in stone rather than the earlier brick and stucco.

The finest house in Cairo

The **Bayt al-Suhaymi** (339) is not a palace and not a refuge for an English major's bric-a-brac. It is a merchant's house of the Ottoman period, built in the 16th and 17th C, and completely furnished to the age. It is the finest house in Cairo and wonderfully achieves the ambition of Islamic secular architecture—the anticipation of paradise. You reach it by taking the first right a block after the Mosque of al-Aqmar. The street is called Haret ed-Darb el Asfar and the house is at No. 19 (in case you do not notice the little green and white plaque) on the left-hand side. There is a broad wooden door. Knock.

There is nothing at the facade that prepares you for what lies within. The house consists of numerous rooms on irregular levels, mashrabiyya screen windows looking out onto the streets at one side, screened and latticed windows and arched galleries giving onto a garden courtyard on the other. You will want to wander, to enjoy the perspectives across the court from every possible angle and elevation, though you will probably be guided—by well-informed students. They will take you, for example, to the women's bedroom which faces the street but is closely latticed, to the women's chapel outside it, a malqaf 'air conditioner' above your head. You will then be deposited in the harem reception room overlooking the garden, its floors of marble, its walls covered with the most delicate green and blue plant-patterned enamel tiles, and with carved and painted wood decorations. Here you can rest and perhaps send out for tea, and begin taking it all in. For it is not the plan, not the details, but the ambience of the place that seduces you and you want time.

Though this house was built in later centuries, in ambience it cannot be different from Cairene houses of earlier times, and it becomes obvious why Crusaders crusaded—the East offered such a luxuriantly pleasurable life for those with the means, far exceeding anything back in Europe. Medieval Western architecture and certainly domestic living (with the possible exception of Provence) was crude in comparison and worst of all uncomfortable. In Europe there were the seasons of cold and wet to contend with; in Egypt the heat. But here in this house they so easily defeated heat and burning sun, creating shadows and breezes, bringing plants and birds into their home, embracing a nature they had made kinder.

The Mosque of al-Hakim and the Northern Gates

Return once again to Sharia Muizz and turn right (north). It becomes wonderful walking along this seemingly humble street, learning its secrets, its treasures offered in this guide still only a sampling of the many more that would require a far longer exploration. You are heading towards Bab al-Futuh and the walls which limit the Fatimid city. But first, on your left, is the clean, pencil-like minaret of the **Silahdar mosque**, a Turkish-style structure of Mohammed

Turkish minaret

Ali's time. Though centuries out of place for this quarter, the minaret is a graceful landmark that never fails to draw your attention as you pass by.

After about two blocks, the street broadens into a market area where garlic and onions are transported into the city and sold. The trucks which rumble in and out of Bab al-Futuh are painted with eyes as talismans against the evil eye. It is an appropriate place for superstition: on your right and leading to the Fatimid wall is the **Mosque of al-Hakim** (15), completed in 1010.

Al-Hakim was the third of the Fatimid caliphs who ruled with absolute political, military and religious authority. He was a paranoic who declared himself God and answered objections by inciting mobs to burn half the city while he lopped off the heads of the well-to-do, claiming the assistance of Adam and Solomon in angel guise. Jews he made walk about Cairo wearing clogs round their necks and Christians he made carry heavy crosses. He would spend his wary nights riding a donkey, in the company of only a mute slave, into the Moqattam to observe the stars for portents. Then exchanging clothes with his slave he would secretly descend into the city and mix with the people to learn their complaints, though assuming the role of a qadi to punish infractions with summary decapitations. One night, returning from the hills, he was assassinated — at the instigation, it is thought, of his sister Setalmulq, whom he had intended to marry.

Some say he survived the attack and retreated to the desert. The Copts claim that Christ appeared to him, and that he begged for and was granted pardon. Others say he withdrew to the sanctuary of Ammon at the Siwa Oasis deep in the Western Desert, where more than a thousand years earlier Alexander had heard himself declared the son of Zeus. There it is said, al-Hakim formulated his doctrine of a tolerant religion, similar to Islam, which was carried by Darazi, his disciple, to Lebanon where the Druze view al-Hakim's life as a kind of Passion, giving him his due as their messiah.

Druze messiah

For centuries this mosque had an aura avoided by Cairenes who rarely used it for worship and let it crumble. It had been used as a prison for Crusader captives, as a stable by Saladin and as a warehouse by Napoleon. As recently as 1980 it was ruinous, its roofless arcades haunting, dominated by its massive brooding minarets in keeping with the Fatimid wall. These minarets proved unsound soon after construction and needed buttressing by great trapeziod bases that project out into the street, so that they seem like ziggurats (especially when viewed from outside the walls), with pepperpot domes, placed there by Baybars II at the begining of the 14th C. The mosque has

Looking across the Mosque of al-Hakim from Bab al-Futuh

now been entirely restored — perhaps over-restored — by the Indian-based Bohra sect of Ismailis who claim spiritual descent from the Fatimid imams. They will tell you that al-Hakim was not mad, that these are the lies of his enemies. And here certainly they have erased the darkness: there is the bright glitter of white marble and gold leaf, and at night the once forbidding arcades are illuminated by the warm glow of suspended glass oil lamps.

The return of the Mecca pilgrimage

It was at **Bab al-Futuh,** the Gate of Conquests, that the great caravan of pilgrims returned each year from Mecca and then made its way along Sharia Muizz and Sharia Bab el Wazir to the Citadel. Nowadays the journey is made by jet, but in 1844 Gérard de Nerval, in *Journey to the Orient*, witnessed it like this: 'As many as 30,000 people were about to swell the population of Cairo. I managed to make my way to Bab al-Futuh; the whole of the main street which leads there was crammed with bystanders who were kept in orderly lines by government troops. The sound of trumpets, cymbals and drums directed the advancing procession; the various nations and sects were distinguished by their trophies and flags. The long files of harnessed dromedaries, which were mounted by Bedouins armed with long rifles, followed one another, but it was only when I reached the countryside that I was able to appreciate the full impact of a spectacle which is unique in all the world.

79

'A whole nation on the march was merging into the huge population which adorned the knolls of the Moqattam on the right, and, on the left, the thousands of usually deserted edifices of the City of the Dead; streaked with red and yellow bands, the turreted copings of the walls and towers of Saladin were also swarming with onlookers. I had the impression that I was present at a scene during the Crusades. Farther ahead, in the plain where the Qalish meanders, stood thousands of chequered tents where the pilgrims halted to refresh themselves; there was no lack of dancers and singers; all the musicians of Cairo, in fact, competed with the hornblowers and kettledrummers of the procession, an enormous orchestra whose members were perched on top of camels.

'Late in the afternoon, the booming of the Citadel cannons and a sudden blast of trumpets proclaimed that the Mahmal, a holy ark which contains Mohammed's robe of golden cloth, had arrived within sight of the city ... From time to time the Mahmal came to a halt, and the entire population prostrated themselves in the dust, cupping their heads in their hands. An escort of guards struggled to drive back the Negroes who were more fanatical than the other Muslims; they aspired, in fact, to the honour of being trampled to death beneath the camels, but the only share of martyrdom bestowed upon them was a volley of baton blows. As for the Santons, who are an even more ecstatic species of saints than the Dervishes and whose orthodoxy is more questionable, several of them pierced their cheeks with long, pointed nails and walked on, showered in blood; others devoured live serpents, while a third group stuffed their mouths with burning coals.'

Nerval was a precursor of surrealism; he enjoyed going over the top. But in this case that sober chronicler Edward William Lane (*Manners and Customs of the Modern Egyptians*), who observed the arrival of the caravan ten years before, is hardly less fantastic in his description, though he says the swallowing of serpents went out with the Mamelukes. The journey from Mecca took 37 days across rocky desert, the caravan moving at night. Not everyone survived: 'Many of the women who go forth to meet their husbands or sons receive the melancholy tidings of their having fallen victim to privation and fatigue. The piercing shrieks with which they rend the air, as they retrace their steps to the city, are often heard predominant over the noise of the drum and the shrill notes of the hautboy which proclaim the joy of others.'

Lane also mentions that the Mahmal was empty; its purpose was entirely symbolic, dating back to the reign of Shagarat al-Durr. She went on the pilgrimage one year, travelling in a magnificent *hodag* or covered litter borne by a camel, and for several successive years her empty hodag was sent with the caravan merely for the sake of state. The practice was continued by Egypt's rulers till 1927, when the puritanical Saudi king, on the pretext of objecting to the soldiers accompanying it, forbade passage of this 'object of vain pomp'. These days, alas, you wait in vain for pomp at Bab al-Futuh.

Along the walls   The gate is similar to Bab Zuwayla, with projecting oval towers, though the masonry is finer and the impression greater for the space outside it has been cleared and there is a magnificent view of the ensemble of **Bab al-Futuh, Bab al-Nasr**—the Gate of Victory—(to the east), the linking **Fatimid wall** and al-Hakim's minarets. The Fatimid wall extends to the west; beyond that, where it retreats, and also to the east of Bab al-Nasr, the wall dates from Saladin. You can walk both within and along the top of the wall between the gates, and to do this you should make yourself obviously interested at either gate and eventually someone with the key will come along.

Re-entering the medieval city through Bab al-Nasr, the immediate area is noisy with metal workshops. On the right (west) against the east facade of al-Hakim's mosque is the caravanserai or **wakala of Sultan Qaytbay** (11) built in 1481. It is now inhabited by tinsmiths and their families; women scrubbing, washing strung across the courtyard, children beating a kitten and throwing it into the air.

PRACTICAL INFORMATION

To reach the starting point of this tour take a **taxi** or the **No. 66 bus** to Khan el Kahlili.

Entrance **fees** are payable at the Qalaun complex and the Bayt al-Suhaymi, and baksheesh should be paid for services elsewhere.

For those with limited time, an **abbreviated itinerary** should include a visit to the Qalaun complex, the Bayt al-Suhaymi and a walk along the walls between Bab al-Futuh and Bab al-Nasr—but above all visit the Bayt al-Suhaymi.

THE CITY OF THE DEAD

The Northern Cemetery or City of the Dead lies to the east of the Fatimid city. The Mausoleum of Barquq is one and a half kilometres from Bab al-Nasr, for example, and Qaytbay's mausoleum is a kilometre from al-Azhar. So a walk from Bab al-Nasr, visiting these two maausolea as well as that of Ashraf Baybars'—the three most outstanding buildings—and then back to al-Azhar, will cover about 3 km. You may prefer to make a separate journey of it, hiring a taxi.

You may already have noticed the City of the Dead as you drove in on the Heliopolis road from the airport; it did not seem inviting. It has the look of a bidonville—hot, dusty, dilapidated, with a quanity of domes. It is in fact the burial ground of the Mameluke sultans and of others who aspired to their end, and some of its mausolea are as wonderful as anything in the city of the living. Nor is the cemetery without life. There were monasteries and schools, part of the mausolea. And the poor have always made their homes here, and the keepers, while relatives visit the family plots on feast days for a picnic. This is reminiscent of the ancient Egyptian practice of feeding the dead, though it is practiced elsewhere in the Mediterranean, as in Greece where it is more a cheerful popping of the cork and celebration of life.

The Three Most Outstanding Mausolea

Follow the road that runs east outside Bab al-Nasr and on reaching the cemetery you will see ahead of you a broad building with two domes and two minarets. This is the **Mausoleum of Barquq** (149), completed in 1411. Its plan is similar to that of a cruciform madrasa, but the liwans are not vaulted, instead entered through multi-domed arcades. You enter nowadays at the southwest corner and pass through a corridor into the sahn, its vastness once relieved by a pair of tamarisk trees, now only by the fountain. On the eastern side is the sanctuary liwan with a beautifully carved marble minbar, dedicated by Qaytbay. At either end of the liwan are domed tomb chambers, Barquq (removed here from his mausoleum in Sharia Muizz) and his two sons buried in the left chamber, women of the family in the right. These domes are the earliest of stone in Cairo; the zigzag ribbing on their exteriors was to develop into the elaborate polygons of Qaytbay's domed mausoleum. From the outside, the domes are minimised by the surrounding structure, and so inside their marvellous shape and soaring height comes as a surprise.

Go back across the courtyard to the northwest corner and

up the stairs. These lead you to the *khanqah* or Dervish monastery, its four storeys a warrren of rooms, cells and corridors. For some extra baksheesh the keeper will usually let you go up the northern minaret for a sweeping view of the nercropolis itself and all of Cairo from Heliopolis to the Citadel.

The **Mausoleum of Sultan Ashraf Baybars** (121)—he is also known as Barsbey—is south down the paved but dusty road that passes along the front of Barquq's mausoleum. This building is less visited than the other two and finding the keeper may be more difficult; at any monument, here or in the city, apprehend the first child or lounger you see and make it known you want the key—the keeper will usually soon appear. Baksheesh is then of course expected all round.

This was originally planned solely as a khanqah and so is unusually elongated; also it is recognised by its ungainly minaret which too soon comes to a point. This Baybars, whose mausoleum dates from 1432, was a Burgi or Circassian Mameluke and is not to be confused with his namesake who held St Louis to ransom. He neither drank nor swore, though was martial enough and took Cyprus from the Franks in 1426. The appeal of the place is in its few but well-chosen elaborations—the polygonally decorated dome rising above the simple facade through which you pass by a doorway with trefoil arch. The tomb chamber is at the north end of the mosque, dimly illuminated by stained-glass windows subsequently introduced, though the mihrab of mother-of-pearl and marble mosaic is original. But really you have come for the interior view of the dome and its impression alone is sufficient: it ascends effortlessly upwards, almost losing itself to infinity.

A jewel of Mameluke architecture

It is a longer distance down this same dusty road to the **Mausoleum of Qaytbay** (99), completed in 1474 and a jewel of Mameluke architecture. First, from across the square, look at the ablaq masonry of the facade, the intricate polygonal relief on the exquisitely proportioned dome, and the slender minaret of three tiers (the Mameluke fashion), each tier ornately decorated with columned recesses or raised arabesques or stalactite clusters. Along with the Ibn Tulun and the Sultan Hassan, this rates as one of the great buildings of Cairo. Unlike them it is free with decoration, but like them it uses its decoration to the highest effect—the frequent play, for example, of filigree flowers upon star-shaped polygons which has been described as 'a song for two voices', a geometrical base with floral melody.

Along with al-Nasr, Qaytbay was the grandest of Mameluke builders, emblazoning his cartouche on buildings religious and secular throughout the Middle East, as well as in Cairo and Alexandria. He was also the last Mameluke

ruler of strength. Meshullam ben Menahem, an Italian
Jew, described him: 'He is an old man of about 80, but tall,
handsome and as upright as a reed. Dressed in white, he
was on horseback, accompanied by more than 2000 Mameluke soldiers ... Whoever wishes can have access to the
sultan: there is in the town a great and splendid fortress at
the entrance of which he sits publicly on Mondays and
Thursdays, accompanied by the governor of the city; a
guard of more than 3000 Mamelukes surrounds him. Whoever has been manhandled or robbed by one of the Mameluke princes or emirs can there complain. Thus the nobles
refrain from actions that might carry condemnation'. He

Tombs in the City of the Dead, c. 1800

came up through the ranks, having been bought by Ashraf Baybars, and apart from al-Nasr ruled longer than any other Sultan. The perfection of his mausoleum, however, like the splendour of his reign, marked the final apogee of Mameluke vigour. Decadence ensued; two decades later the Turks were in the city, Bab Zuwayla ornamented by the last Mameluke sultan, a rope round his neck.

Inside is a cruciform madrasa with vestigial liwans to east and west. The decoration of ceilings, pavings, arches, windows is breathtakingly variegated, yet overall it is measured and subdued. There is deliberate though sensitive contrast with the scale of the courtyard and sanctuary in the immense height of the tomb chamber, its walls drawn into the ascending dome.

Finally, from the sanctuary, you should climb the roof to enjoy at closer hand the tracery of stone carving, as delicate as previous periods had managed in wood and stucco, on the dome and minaret.

PRACTICAL INFORMATION

Apart from resorting to a **taxi, bus No. 500** from Midan el Tahrir to Midan el Barquq; the Mausoleum of Barquq lies not far to the southeast.

For those with limited time the temptation might be to leave out this long journey to the City of the Dead altogether, but even the most **abbreviated itinerary** should include a visit to the Mausoleum of Qaytbay, one of the finest enclosed interiors in the world.

THE EGYPTIAN MUSEUM

The Museum of Egyptian Antiquities, to give it its proper name, is on the north side of the Midan el Tahrir, near the Nile Hilton. It was founded at Bulaq in 1858 by Auguste Mariette, the great pioneer archaeologist who first excavated the Serapeum at Saqqara, the Temple of Amun at Karnak, Hatshepsut's mortuary temple at Deir el Bahri, and the temples at Dendera and Edfu. The collection has occupied the present classical-style building since 1902 and has long since outgrown it. There are over 100,000 exhibits which could easily fill half a dozen museums this size, a unique storehouse of one of the oldest and grandest civilisations on earth.

Allowing one minute for each exhibit, you could see everything in the museum in about nine months. The average guided tour lasts two hours. The selection offered here would take one hard-working day to cover, though it would be better to break that down into two or three half-day visits.

The exhibits are numbered and some carry background notes in English, French and Arabic. The rooms are also numbered, as shown on the plans. The collection is arranged more or less chronologically, so that starting at the entrance and walking clockwise round the ground floor you pass from Old Kingdom through Middle and New Kingdom exhibits, concluding with Ptolemaic and Roman exhibits. The first floor contains prehistoric and early dynastic exhibits and the contents of several tombs, including Tutankhamun's. *Not every room is mentioned in the tour below.*

The Ground Floor
Immediately upon entering (from the south), you walk into a rotunda that is *Room 48*. Apart from the monumental Sphinx at Giza, the colossal head to the left (6051) of Userkaf (V Dyn) is the only large sculpture surviving from the Old Kingdom. The rotunda contains other giant works (out of chronological order), including three colossi (1, 2, 4) of Ramses II (XIX Dyn) and a statue of Amenhotep son of Hapu (3), architect to Amenophis III (XVIII Dyn).

The Old Kingdom *Room 47*: Contains IV, V and VI Dynasty items. The walls are lined with sarcophagi. Most interesting are the figures in the central aisle cases, including, in Case B, statuettes of the dwarf (160), the man with a deformed head (6310) and the hunchback (6311), but also, in Case D, those of people grinding corn, kneading dough, preparing food (a goose about to be gutted and plucked).

Room 41: The V Dynasty bas-relief (79) with scenes of country life is particularly worthy of close observation. Farm tasks and crafts are carried on through a series of registers. The women wear ankle-length chemises, but the men wear only a cloth or are sometimes entirely naked. They are circumcised as was the Egyptian custom. There is also one episode of a malefactor being held and brought before a court.

Room 42: The very fine statue of Chephren (138) in black diorite with white marbling was found in a shaft at his Valley Temple at Giza where he built the second of the Great Pyramids. The falcon god Horus embraces Chephren's head with his wings, at once transferring the ka and protecting the pharaoh. The remarkably preserved wooden statue of Ka-aper (140) is vividly executed. You feel you would recognise the face in the original, and indeed when Mariette found it at Saqqara his workmen immediately dubbed it Sheikh el Beled because of its resemblance to their village headman. The living eyes are copper inlaid with quartz. It is said of some paintings that the eyes follow you; in this case it is uncanny how they fix you with their sure and level gaze when faced head on, but as soon as you shift even a centimetre they gaze off — not inert, but reflectively, into an internal dream world of their past.

Room 31: Outstanding here are the six wooden panels of the II Dynasty priest Hesire (88). This was the brief period in ancient Egyptian history when moustaches were fashionable.

Room 32: One gets so used to the rigid frontality of Egyptian sculpture that it is a surprise to see the wooden statue in the far right corner with its slight twist. At the centre of the room are the IV Dynasty statues (223, 195) of Prince Rahotep and Princess Nafrit, her skin painted yellow, his ruddy brown. He has short back and sides and sports a natty moustache. In his white waist cloth he looks all the world like an advertising executive taking a sauna. The group representing the dwarf Seneb, Chief of the Wardrobe, with his wife and two children (6055) deserves close attention. It is delightful, but also a puzzle. Despite his small size, Seneb is a man of importance; he looks pleased with himself, sure of his position, his family, his wife's proud affection. Notice his legs: they are too short to hang over the edge of the chair; instead his children stand where his legs would be — is this a mere compositional nicety or has it a symbolic intention? And look at the children, their right index fingers to their lips as though they were keeping a secret. The III/IV Dynasty 'Geese of Meidum' (136) are vividly coloured. The copper statues (230, 231) of Pepi I and his son are the first metal statues known, and that of Pepi the largest of its kind. He is a great striding figure, reminiscent of an archaic Greek kouros.

The Middle Kingdom
With *Room 26* you pass into the Middle Kingdom.

Room 22: Generally sculpture and stone monuments of

First floor

		Jewels		
1	2	3	4 Tutankhamun	5
6	7	8	9 Tutankhamun	10
11	12	13	14	15
16	17		19	20
21	22		24	25
26	27		29	30
31	32		34	35
36	37		39	40
41	42	43	44	45

Tutankhamun

| 51 | 46 | 47 | 48 | 49 | 50 | 57 |

| 52 Mummy Room | 53 | 54 | 55 | 56 |

Ground floor

		3 Akhenaton		
1	2		4	5
6	7	8	9	10
11	12	13	14	15
16	17	18	19	20
21	22	23 Atrium	24	25
26	27	28	29	30
31	32	33	34	35
36	37	38	39	40
41	42	43	44	45

WC

| 46 | 47 | 48 Rotunda | 49 | 50 |

WC

Shop

Entrance

the Middle Kingdom. At the centre is the burial chamber of Horhotep (300). The walls are painted with oil jars and offerings are closely listed. The decorated doors, like patchwork curtains, were for the ka to flit in and out at will. Around the chamber are ten statues of Sesostris I (301). On the sides of each throne are reliefs of the gods of Upper and Lower Egypt entwining the lotus and papyrus, symbolising the unity of the country.

The New Kingdom   With *Room 11* you pass into the New Kingdom. 400: a fine statue of Tuthmosis III (XVII Dynasty) in grey schist.

Room 12: XVIII Dynasty sculpture. The brightly decorated chapel built for Amenophis II or his predecessor Tuthmosis III once contained Hathor as cow (445, 446) — she now stands before it in a glass case. To the right is a pink granite statue (952) of Hatshepsut. Look also for the case containing a small statuette (6257), delicately carved out of Sudanese ebony, of Thay, a royal equerry.

Room 8: It is unusual for mud brick houses, even palaces, to survive, and so our impression of ancient Egypt is largely determined, often distorted, by rock tombs and stone mortuary temples. But the Egyptians did concern themselves with this world and at the centre of this room is a model of a typical house as excavated at Tell el Amarna, Akhenaton's brief capital on the Nile near Minya.

The Akhenaton Room   *Room 3* contains perhaps the most astonishing works in the museum, from the reign of Akhenaton. Some find the Amarna style — particularly when applied in its most exaggerated form to Akhenaton himself — grotesque. I think it powerful and often beautiful. Staring down at you are four colossi of the pharaoh: the glare of revolution. Elongated face, narrow eyes, long thin nose with flaring nostrils and full, perhaps sardonic lips. The belly and thighs protrude like some primitive female fertility figure. These are from the temple he built, at Karnak, later destroyed, its blocks serving as foundations and pylon filler for others' works. In its own glass case there is a magnificent head, probably of Nefertiti, and this is not distorted at all — though examples of Amarnan distortion applied to Nefertiti are seen on the stele in Case F, and the centre stele in Case H. This distortion is sometimes called realism; there is a theory that Akhenaton was indeed deformed and that some of his family may have been also — and that the Amarna style was a mass acquiescence to this misfortune. But you might prefer to think that this style was deliberately experimental, calculated for effect, indeed to illustrate opposition, and as readily dispensed with (as with the bust of Nefertiti, above) when sheer beauty rather than shock value was desired. There *is* a note of realism, at least intimacy, in the centre stele in Case F. Instead of showing the royal family in formal adoration of the sun disc Aton,

Akhenaton (Room 3): the glare of revolution

Akhenaton is seen playing with his eldest daughter Meritaten, while Nefertiti holds their other two daughters on her lap. This expression of family joy, or any personal feelings whatsoever, was seen never before and never again in depictions of the pharaohs. Note also the cuneiform tablets, the famous 'Amarna Letters', in Case A, and the representational masks, either models or perhaps death masks, eg 478 in Case D.

Coins *Room 4* contains a collection of Greek, Roman, Byzantine and Arab coins. Quite a few bear the head of Alexander, and on the left side of the first case on the right are several coins bearing the head of Cleopatra VII.

The Ramessids *Room 15*: Items from the reign of Ramses II, including a painted limestone statue of a XIX Dynasty queen from the Ramesseum (Case A).

Room 14: On the right is a statue (743) of Ramses VI (XX Dyn), unusual for its attempt at movement, dragging a doubled up Libyan by the hair. A painted sunk relief (769) in the left near corner shows Ramses II similarly apprehending three prisoners, one black, one red, one brown. At the centre (unnumbered, but catalogued as 765) is a unique freestanding coronation group sculpture, Ramses III at the centre, Horus on the left, Seth on the right. Though greatly restored, enough was found to determine that the figures stood on their own legs without supports.

The Late Period The New Kingdom, in any case tottering since the end of the XX Dynasty, ended with the XXI Dynasty. Objects from the Late Period begin with *Room 25*. One ruler of the XXV Dynasty, Taharka, left his mark at several sites in Upper Egypt, eg the remains of his kiosk in the Great Court at Karnak. Here you see his sculpted head (1185) with curled hair—he was from the Sudan (which the Greeks called Ethiopia). He enjoys the distinction of being mentioned in the Bible (II Kings 19:9). In *Room 24* is a green schist statue of the goddess Tweri (791)—finely finished, though an utterly ridiculous image of a pregnant anthropomorphic hippopotamus. Otherwise, the most interesting items are the Osiris, Isis and Hathor group (855, 856, 857) at the centre, and to the left 1184, an attempt at portraiture of the Mayor of Thebes.

Room 30: At Medinet Habu are the mortuary chapels of the Divine Adorers of Amun. Amenardis, in white stone (930), was one of these princesses, of the XXV Dynasty.

The Graeco-Roman Period *Room 34*: Note the colossal bust (1003) of Serapis. This god was an invention of Ptolemy Soter and combined Osiris with Apis, the bull god of Memphis, but with Greek features and dress.

Room 44: The contents of royal tombs of a Nubian people, the Blemmyes, who lived just south of Abu Simbel during the Byzantine period and were under the dominion of

Meroë in the Sudan. Their aristocracy was strongly negroid. Long after Christianity came to Egypt, they worshipped Isis, Horus and Bes. The burial of kings and queens was accompanied by strangled slaves and servants, and gaily caparisoned horses which were led into the tombs and axed to death. Crowns, the skeleton of a horse, the caparisoned models of two others, along with spearheads, jewellery, pottery and other artefacts form this fascinating exhibit. The artefacts of the Blemmyes have a strong, handsome look, similar to Celtic work — a fine brutality.

Room 49: An exceptional piece is the coffin of Petosiris (6036), a high priest of Thoth at Hermopolis (c.300 BC). The hieroglyphs are beautifully inlaid with stone and enamel. From Saqqara during the Persian Period is the stone sarcophagus (on the right, near the rotunda) of a dwarf dancer at the Serapeum Apis ceremony. He has been well rewarded: his true to life figure is cut on the outside of the adjacent lid, while on the inside of the lid and at the bottom of the sarcophagus is carved a sex-bomb Nut for him to lie on and stare up at for eternity.

The Atrium: large objects of various periods

On the ground floor there now remains only the atrium to visit.

At the centre of *Room 43* is the Palette of Narmer (3055), possibly the oldest record of a political event, the unification of Egypt, c.3100 BC. Narmer was probably one of the names of Menes, the founder of the I Dynasty, from which Egypt's historical period is dated. Writing was not yet able to convey complex sentences and this slate palette tells its story by means of pictures which are easily translated into words. On the obverse, Narmer is shown braining an enemy, and to the right is a complex symbol relating the significance of this action. The falcon is Narmer, holding a rope attached to the head of a bearded man. The head protrudes from a bed of papyri, representing Lower Egypt. Therefore the symbol reads, 'The falcon god Horus (Narmer) leads captive the inhabitants of the papyrus country'. Narmer came from Upper Egypt, as the crown he wears on this side shows. On the reverse, Narmer wears the crown of Lower Egypt as he reviews the spoils of his victory, which include the decapitated bodies of his foes. The centre panel shows two fantastic beasts, their necks entwined but restrained from fighting by bearded men on either side: Upper and Lower Egypt joined, if not yet altogether at ease. On either side of the room are two large wooden boats for solar sailing from the pyramid of Sesostris III at Dahshur.

Room 38 is really a stairway leading down into the well of the atrium and contains the rectangular stone sarcophagus (624) of Ay, at first an advisor to Akhenaton and later his successor. Four goddesses at each corner extend their wings protectively: Isis, Nephthys, Neith and Selket.

Room 33 displays various pyramidions from Dahshur, the capstones to pyramids. Under 6175 you can see the stone peg which slotted into the pyramid top. The sarcophagus (6337A) of Psusennas I, a XXI Dynasty pharaoh ruling from Tanis in the Delta after Egypt had split in two, has its lid (6337B) raised over a mirror so that you can see the lovely raised relief of Nut suspended from its underside. To the left, from the XVIII Dynasty, are the stone sarcophagi of Tuthmosis I (619), that of his daughter Hatshepsut made before she came to the throne (6024) and her final sarcophagus (620).

At the centre of the atrium (*Room 28*) is a painted floor with a river scene (627) from the palace of Akhenaton at Tell el Amarna.

In *Room 23* there are two interesting lintels, the one on the left (6189) showing the Heb-Sed of Senusret III (XII Dyn) very finely cut in sunk relief, while the one on the right is a tenth-rate copy by a later pharaoh.

Room 18 (the stairway leading out of the atrium well) has the colossal group (610) of Amenophis III and his wife Tiy with three of their daughters (XVII Dyn). They are serene, almost a portrait of Victorian contentment but for the play of a smile on their lips and the physicalness of their bodies. Despite the formality of the work and its size, there is a great sensuality to it. The reign of Amenophis was marked by luxury and a sudden eruption (or at least recording) of fashion consciousness: note particularly Tiy's full wig, the hair falling down to her breasts, a style associated almost exclusively with this reign.

Room 13: On the right is a fascinating document, a stele (599) inscribed on the reverse during the reign of Amenophis III with all that the pharaoh had done for Amun, but later inscribed on the obverse by Merneptah, pharaoh at about the time of the Exodus, with the sole known reference in Egyptian texts to the Israelites: 'Israel is crushed, it has no more seed!'

The *corridors* on either side of the atrium (allowing communication between Rooms 43 and 8 but not with the atrium itself) are lined with pottery, wall paintings and inscription fragments.

The First Floor

To see the first floor rooms in approximate chronological order you should start at Room 43 overlooking the atrium from the south and follow the corridors in a clockwise direction.

Old and Middle Kingdom tomb contents

Outside *Room 42* is a panel (6278) inlaid with blue faience, from Zoser's Step Pyramid at Saqqara. Inside the room you should spend time with the alabaster vase (3054) on the right, beautifully round and smooth and yet criss-crossed in raised stone with ropes from which it would have been suspended. In Case Q is the black Palermo Stone which bears a list of pharaohs from the I to mid-V Dynasties along with important events during the period and annual measurements of the Nile flood, thus adding to our knowledge of the Old Kingdom.

Room 37 is full of wooden coffins and sarcophagi of the Middle Kingdom. The coffin of Sepi (3101 in Case C), a XII Dynasty general, is particularly well-painted. This is the oldest anthropoid coffin in the museum. See also the dismantled panels of his sarcophagus (3104 in Cases A and L), finely painted and extensively inscribed. Artefacts from the tomb of General Mesah at Assiut are displayed in several cases and include his sandals, mirror and neck pillow, and models of Egyptian soldiers (3345), black soldiers (3346) and a pleasure barge (3347).

In the corridor facing *Room 32* is a rare and astonishing wooden ka statue (280) of the Pharaoh Hor (XII Dyn) stepping out from its naos. It actually stands on a sliding base to demonstrate the wanderings of Hor's double — and that it is his ka is clear from the ka hieroglyph of upraised arms on his head, and his nakedness. Inside the room are models (Case E: 3246, 4347) of solar boats. The solar boats are unmanned, operating on autopilot. They are the abstraction of the other boats displayed: funerary boats for carrying the dead man on a canopied bier, or for transport of the living. There is a delightful model of a boat (3244 in Case F) with its mast down, its rowers pulling at full strength, one rower taking a quick sidelong glance at you as the boat shoots by.

Room 27 contains marvellous models (6077–86) from the XI Dynasty tomb of Meketre at Thebes, including a plantation owner reviewing a parade of his cattle and workers (6080); a carpenters' workshop (6083); a pleasure garden with pool, lined with sycamore-figs, at one end a columned verandah (6084); and two boats dragging a net between them, taking fish from the Nile (6085).

New Kingdom tomb contents

Room 22 contains many interesting small figures, including XII–XXX Dynasty ushabtis (Cases I and J: 6062–72), and women, perhaps concubines of the dead man, lying on beds (Case C: 9435, 9437). Cases O, P and R contain New Kingdom funerary gear, painted linen or woven cloth for covering the chest, body and feet, beautifully designed and all the more fine for being highly perishable materials that have survived.

Room 17 is particularly interesting for the papyri on its walls from the Book of the Dead.

Room 12 contains artefacts from royal tombs: a chariot of Tuthmosis IV (3000); the mummies of a child and a gazelle (Case I: 3776, 3780); a collection of priestly wigs and wig boxes (Case L: 3779).

Room 13 at the north end of the atrium displays furnishings from the intact Theban tomb of Yuya and Tuyu, parents-in-law of Amenophis III, with beds, chairs, whippet-like chariots, mummified food and time-serving ushabtis.

The north end of the first floor and all the outer rooms along its east side are devoted to Tutankhamun's treasures, but it is not easy to include their profusion in the middle of this tour. Come back to it later. In any case, more affecting are the burial exhibits in *Room 14*. These people, mostly **Graeco-Roman** Greeks from the Fayyum, continued the Egyptian practice **burials** of mummification, yet from their portraits, so lifelike and modern, you cannot imagine they would have accepted the ancient belief. The encaustic portraits (colours mixed into molten wax) were bound onto the mummies—there are shelves of these. A collection of panels is against the south wall (4310): the technique is superb, with shading, highlighting and perspective, two or three of them qualifying as masterpieces in their own right. Those garbage bodies, yet these living faces in which you can read whole lives. All are marked by a seriousness, rarely pompous, occasionally sad, a faint smile on one man's lips. They have steadfastly faced the passing millenia and now look at you as you look at them as though suddenly we might recognise one another.

In *Room 19* are the gods of the Egyptian pantheon.

Room 24 is full of painted ostraka, limestone fragments. **Sketches,** Case 18 contains interesting representations of animals: a **papyri and** monkey eating, a man leading a bull, a lion devouring a **decorations** prisoner, etc. People too: an intriguing picture of a woman relaxing and playing a stringed instrument. There is also, in the east doorway, a plan of a Theban tomb (4371), with what appear to be doorways shown in elevation.

In *Room 29* are further ostraka, but written on, and papyri—6335 especially worthwhile: a Ptolemaic Book of the Dead in finest detail, showing the 'Weighing of the Heart' ceremony.

In the corridor outside *Room 34* is an Amarna toilet seat. Is this the loo on which Akhenaton sat?

Room 44 displays decorative details, most interesting the faience from palaces of Ramses II and III.

Room 57 is around the southeast staircase. The square red and green leather tent (3848) belonged to a XXI Dynasty queen and was used at her funeral.

At the centre of the south wings is *Room 48* with a model of a funerary complex, showing how a river temple linked with the pyramid on the desert's edge. There is also a cross-sectioned pyramid showing the internal buttressing. A case to the north contains beautifully worked statuettes from various periods.

Prehistoric and *Rooms 54, 55 and 53* are devoted to prehistoric and pre-**predynastic** dynastic artefacts, eg pottery and tools, and are generally **periods** dull, except that in *Room 53* are mummified baboons, a dog,

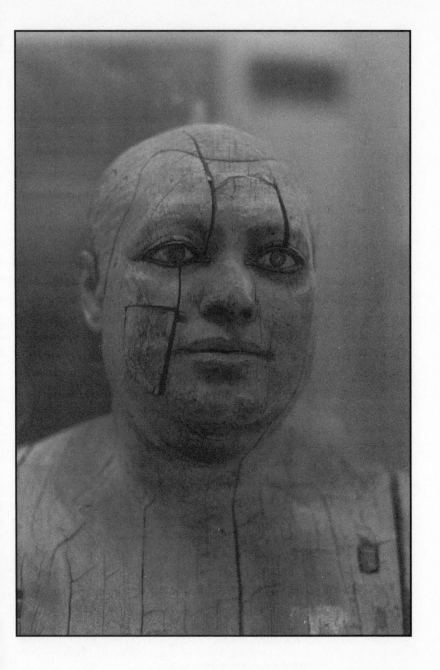

Sheikh el Beled (Room 42): internal dream world

a crocodile and the skeleton of a mare—and these are disgusting. You can understand that the Egyptians, having convinced themselves of the efficacy of preservation, would wrap each other up. But to impose it on animals (look at their little linen-wrapped legs) seems perverse. This is perhaps an unfair view, for human beings are at the centre of our cosmology, animals only soulless lookers-on, while Egyptian religion grew out of animal worship, totemism, an admiration of their qualities (strength, swiftness, beauty), or a desire to appease; wild dogs, the 'Egyptian wolf', prowled the cemeteries by night in search of bones and bodies that the Egyptians hoped would remain unmolested, and so this predator of their eternal life was transformed into their funerary deity, Anubis. Animal cults proliferated towards the end of the pagan period and were extremely popular, religious societies collecting the sacred animals (from shrew mice to hippopotami) which died in the district, mummifying them and burying them in special cemeteries.

The Mummy Room

Room 52 is the Mummy Room where many of the mightiest men in ancient history lie naked and bird-boned in glass cases. Alas, since early 1981 visitors have been forbidden entry. The royal bodies of Amenophis III, Seti I, Ramses II and others are to be reburied either in their original tombs or in a chamber built for the purpose. This is meant as a gesture to Islam, though only the most fundamentalist Muslims can have been offended. I am inclined to agree with Jean Cocteau that the pharaohs did not intend to hide away: 'The more I walk along, the more I listen, the more I move around the columns, the more do I experience the feeling of a dark world which fastens on to ours and which will not loosen the suckers through which it takes its life. Whatever it may cost, they find it necessary to confirm their existence, to perpetuate themselves, to incarnate, to reincarnate, to hypnotise nothingness and to vanquish it. . . They did not hide themselves in order to disappear, but in order to await the cue for their entry on the stage. They have not been dragged from the tomb. They have been brought from the limbo of the wings with masks and gloves of gold . . . Seti the First! How beautiful he is, with his little nose, his pointed teeth showing, his little face which belongs to death, reduced to one requirement alone—not to die. "I! I! I!" This is the word which the rafters throw back.'

Returning to the New Kingdom

You can now walk back to the north end of the first floor for the Tutankhamun exhibition which begins at *Room 7*. You pass through *Room 6* with a collection of scarabs. This black dung beetle, running everywhere about the desert sands, pushing a ball of dung before it, symbolised the self-creator, the morning sun.

Rooms 2 and 3, though leading off from the Tutankhamun

exhibition area, are not properly part of it. In *Room 2* is a falcon-style coffin, very impressive in black with gold leaf design and gold bird's face (Case 4).

The Jewellery Room

Room 3 closes a quarter of an hour before the rest of the museum and is specially guarded: it contains jewellery from the I Dynasty through to the Byzantine period: necklaces, pectorals, diadems, daggers and much else in gold, silver and precious stones. The best workmanship is found in the jewellery of the XII Dynasty, and the stones are real (carnelian for red and orange, amethyst for purple and violet, lapis lazuli for blue, feldspar for green)—in Tutankhamun's time, as you will see in the following rooms, paste and glass were used instead and though the settings are gold it is mere costume jewellery. If I could walk out with any of it, you would find the VI Dynasty gold falcon head (Case 3: 4010) missing, and Mary Astor, Peter Lorre and Sidney Greenstreet hot on my trail.

The Tutankhamun Exhibition

Walking round the Tutankhamun exhibition, you occasionally notice a dust-free silhouette where a piece has been removed to join one of the Tut Tours around America, Britain, France, etc, and yet these absences hardly relieve the overwhelming impression of the whole. There is just so much, yet Tutankhamun was a minor figure who died young and was stuffed into a small tomb; imagine the impedimenta that Seti I tried taking with him. I have seen three Tutankhamun roadshows and have in each case preferred their careful choice and presentation to the jumble sale effect at the Cairo Museum. *Rooms 7, 8, 9, 10, 15, 25, 30, 35, 40 and 45*, and also *Room 4* (off Room 9) and part of *Room 13*, contain 1700 items in all. The eyes jadedly search for the highlights of the highlights, or otherwise fix on curiosities.

Tutankhamun's mummy, his outermost coffin of gilded wood and his granite sarcophagus are all in his tomb in the Valley of the Kings, but the second coffin of gilded wood and the third of solid gold are in *Room 4*, along with the

The gold mask

gold mask. Each of these, placed one within the other like Russian dolls, in turn were placed within a gilded wood shrine—which again fitted within three more (*Rooms 7 and 8*). These shrines remind me of Wilhelm Reich's orgone boxes, a crackpot device for concentrating orgone energy around the human body: 'Quite unexpectedly the knowledge of the biological function of tension and charge led me to the discovery of hitherto unknown energy processes in bions, in the human organism and in the radiation of the sun... This energy, which is capable of charging nonconducting substances, I termed *orgone*... The orgone energy has a parasympatheticotonic effect and charges living tissues... The human organism is surrounded by an orgonotic field which varies according to the individual's vegetative motility' (Reich, *The Function of the Orgasm*). The ancient Egyptians, however, were born and died too soon to benefit from Reich's teachings, and employed these gold casings in part because gold was thought to be the flesh of the gods, and also because it warded off all outside contamination, presumably including, alas, orgone.

In *Room 5* is a curiosity other examples of which you may have noticed elsewhere in the museum: a vegetating Osiris (Case 93, 1064). It is a wooden silhouette of the god, his image again carved out within this and the depression once filled with earth from which grass would sprout with symbolic effect.

Tutankhamun's throne

Among the finer or more curious items in the east gallery (*Rooms 15 to 45*) are a jewellery casket of gilded wood (*Room 45*, Case 54, 447) in the form of a naos with the figure of Anubis on top; a chest (*Room 35*, Case 20, 324) for the pharaoh's clothes decorated on the lid with a desert hunt, on the large panels with Tutankhamun waging war, and on the small panels with the royal sphinx trampling on his enemies; two life-size statues of Tutankhamun (96 and 181, at the entrance to Room 45 near the stairway) which guarded the entrance to the burial chamber; and the famous small throne (1), its back richly decorated with a scene of Tutankhamun's queen placing her right hand on his left shoulder, often interpreted as a relaxed domestic scene, though probably a gesture confirming his position, as she was after all the daughter — and possibly a widow — of Akhenaton, and the royal ka was transferred through the female line (explaining the frequent sister and daughter marriages of pharaohs). The armrests too are beautiful, the lovely shape of falcons' wings extending in protection, the birds' heads wearing the crown of Upper and Lower Egypt. As you leave the gallery, on either side of the doorway are statues of the two guards who were found standing in Tutankhamun's tomb. It was a job they quietly performed for well over 3000 years until Howard Carter caught them napping. In penance they must stand here in the Cairo Museum for a few more years yet.

PRACTICAL INFORMATION

The Museum of Egyptian Antiquities is open daily from 9am to 4pm except Fridays when it is closed from 11.30 to 1.30. Entrance **fee** is LE3, or LE1.50 for students with card.

For sale at the ticket kiosk is *A Guide to the Egyptian Museum*, LE3. This is the official publication and is reasonably comprehensive though descriptions are perfunctory and it is arranged by catalogue number rather than by room which makes it a nuisance to use. It is probably of little value to the passer-through.

A fee of LE10 is payable if you want to take photographs inside. Otherwise bags and cameras cannot be taken into the museum. These may be checked free of charge (which does not stop the attendant, *sotto voce*, asking for 50PT).

There is a shop just inside the entrance selling books, cards, reproductions, etc.

THE PYRAMID AGE

Before taking the Giza road out to that desert escarpment where the famous Pyramids of Cheops, Chephren and Mycerinus stand, it is worth knowing something of the period in which they were built, and to know too something of that entire line of Old Kingdom pyramids which extends from Abu Roash to the north of Giza to Meidum near the Fayyum, a line that is 70 km long and numbers over 80 pyramids. This chapter will refer to the main pyramid clusters, and will explain why and how, at the very beginning of recorded history, these most prodigious and enduring monuments in stone were built. 'Everything fears time', wrote an Arab physician in the 12th C, 'but time fears the Pyramids'.

The First Pyramid

The struggle for unity

Around 3100 BC, Upper and Lower Egypt were united under Menes and the I Dynasty established. It is not certain that Menes was an individual; he may represent a conflation of early warrior-princes, and the conquest of the Delta may not have been a single campaign but a struggle lasting over generations. There is evidence of fighting and

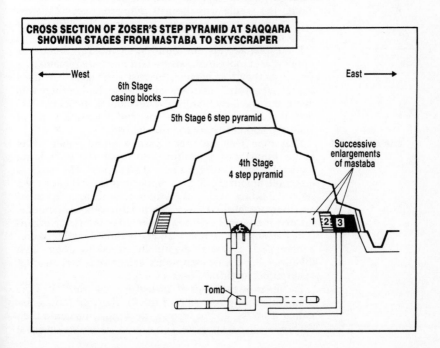

CROSS SECTION OF ZOSER'S STEP PYRAMID AT SAQQARA SHOWING STAGES FROM MASTABA TO SKYSCRAPER

← West   East →

6th Stage casing blocks

5th Stage 6 step pyramid

4th Stage 4 step pyramid

Successive enlargements of mastaba

1 2 3

Tomb

rebellion during the I and II Dynasties, and the energies of this period would have been devoted to consolidation. Building was in mud brick and reed, though during the II Dynasty some stone was used underground in tombs.

Mastabas Below ground these tombs were built like houses: rectangular and divided into chambers. Above ground they had a low, flat-topped form with sloping walls. This mud brick superstructure was sometimes faced with mud plaster and covered with white gypsum stucco. Mariette called them *mastabas*, the Arabic for those stone benches outside the shops and coffee houses of medieval Cairo.

The Old Kingdom About 400 years after unification, that is c.2700 BC, Egypt entered into a long period of security and order known to us as the Old Kingdom and beginning with the III Dynasty. Awareness of the two Egypts, Upper and Lower, remained acute, as can be read from the ritual of Zoser's Heb-Sed festival at Saqqara, and the village and tribal units up and down the Nile continued to worship their local gods, that prolific pantheon that never disappeared but which eventually was overlaid by a few powerful national cults.

The III Dynasty: building in stone During the reign of Zoser (III Dyn) there was a sudden use and mastery of stone at Saqqara. His mortuary complex of courts and chapels, 544 metres long and 277 metres wide and surrounded by a wall 10 metres high, was all of stone, beautifully detailed and architectured. And dominating the whole was the first pyramid, over 62 metres high, built in steps. Stone had risen from the darkness of the tomb into the confident light of the sun.

The explanation is not found in technology; stone was not new and tools and construction methods remained as simple as they had been in the past—the lever was used but the wheel and pulley were unknown. Rather there was peace and stability; there was a developing theocratic doctrine that invited the use of stone; and there was a man of genius who knew how to build with it.

The genius of Imhotep That man was Imhotep, Zoser's grand vizier, chief judge, minister of agriculture and supervisor of building works. He was also high priest at Heliopolis. His range of accomplishment typified the opportunities and needs of a new civilisation, where everything was still to be invented and then organised. He was revered throughout pharaonic history, though recalled as a healer rather than as an organiser, statesman or architect, and he became a mythic figure, a demi-god, and was eventually raised to unqualified divinity—but his contemporary existence is certain from inscriptions found at Zoser's complex.

The doctrine that begged the use of stone was that of the pharaoh's sole possession of the *ka*, the vital force emanating from the god to his son, the king, who could then dispense it to his subjects. The ka was eternal so long as it was linked to the pharaoh, and so it was essential that ka and king be given an indestructible container of stone.

Building the first pyramid

Zoser was built a stone mastaba and this was twice enlarged. Then in three further stages, Imhotep made a qualitative leap, a sudden vertical thrust, and created the world's first skyscraper, the Step Pyramid. Political and cultural revolution in Egypt has always swept down through the valley, nomadic in inspiration. The mastaba belonged to the earthbound world of the Delta farmers; the pyramid and generally Egyptian architecture thereafter eschewed the enclosure of space and instead posed itself against the sun and the stars. Stone permitted it; Imhotep mastered the physics required; and yearning for the vast and timeless cosmos was its inspiration.

It is interesting and important, though, that Zoser's complex remains human in feeling. Zoser was the son of the god, and even if he was the god himself, he at least relished the life of man, for in the house-like arrangement of chambers beneath his pyramid, with their faience decorations imitating domestic reeding, there is the desire to project his present life into the hereafter. This sense never again appears inside a pyramid, and rarely at any mortuary structure of a pharaoh throughout Egypt's history. Instead the savouring of the everyday was excluded, divinity insisted upon, and ritual became obsessive.

The pyramid revolution

So there was a first revolution, an eruption, in stone. But the second revolution was an adventure even more astonishing and led to the perfection of the pyramid form at Giza. We think of the vastness of Egyptian history and how slowly it must have unfolded, yet from Zoser's complex to Cheops' Pyramid no more time passed than our fast-moving age took to travel from the beginnings of iron construction to the Eiffel Tower — around 75 years in fact. What is more, the age of the great pyramids was over in 200 years. What explains its sudden coming and going, and the intensity, the phenomenal labour, with which it was pursued?

You see that in rushing out to Giza you confront the apogee, but you do not meet the answer. That is found to the south of Saqqara, at Dahshur and at Meidum.

The Pyramid Production Line

The collapse of the Meidum pyramid

The pyramid at Meidum is about 90 km by road south of Cairo and even without visiting it you can see it, if you are alert, from the left side of the overnight train back from Luxor soon after it passes El Wasta in the morning. Like all the pyramids, it stands beyond the belt of cultivation on the edge of the desert. It is an amazing sight: a steeply inclined tower rising from a low hill — and that is exactly what it was thought to be by early travellers. In fact it is a pyramid that collapsed. It did not slowly crumble over time; near the moment of its completion there was some catastrophe. Then or after a series of collapses only a part of the core remained clear of the mound of debris all around.

This was the first pyramid after Zoser's and it was conceived at first as a step pyramid. A second, larger stepped structure was soon superimposed and finally a true pyramidal shell was added, its smooth sides rising at an angle of about 52°. But there were serious design faults, including the badly squared stones of the outer casing which stood on horizontal limestone blocks embedded in compacted sand instead of on a bedrock foundation given an inward slope. The weight of the pyramid, instead of being directed downwards and inwards, was directed outwards; it was destroyed by its own lateral forces.

The mystery of Snofru's pyramids at Dahshur This disaster leads to an explanation of the pyramid craze that marks the succeeding dynasty to Zoser's. An inscription at Meidum says it was built by Snofru (IV Dyn). But this has disturbed Egyptologists because Snofru was known to have built two pyramids at Dahshur. If the purpose of a pyramid was to provide an indestructible container for the pharaoh and his ka, why did Snofru need three? Snofru's inscription was explained away as a usurpation of his predecessor's pyramid: 'It cannot but seem extraordinary that one and the same king should have built for himself two pyramids of vast dimensions at no great distance from one another . . . and since it is hard to imagine that he erected three pyramids, the one at Meidum is now tentatively ascribed to Huny', wrote Sir Alan Gardiner, the noted Egyptologist, in *Egypt of the Pharaohs*. But that left the Bent and Red Pyramids at Dahshur. The Bent Pyramid was disposed of with the argument that it had been deemed unsafe and so Snofru decided to build another. One pharaoh, one ka and one pyramid to suit.

The Bent Pyramid rises for 70 percent of its bulk at an angle of 52°, the same as at Meidum. It then abruptly alters angle to 43.5°. The Red Pyramid rises at a constant angle of 43.5°. The lower angle of the Red would clearly be safer than the steeper initial angle of the Bent, but it fails to explain why the angle of the Bent should have been changed in mid-construction. If the steep initial angle of the Bent was thought to be unsafe, why not at once abandon the project? But if changing the angle was thought to make it safe, why build the Red Pyramid? Of course, one could argue that it was thought the change of angle would make the Bent Pyramid safe and that unhappily this proved not to be true—though the pyramid has stood safe and sound for nearly 5000 years.

Eminent Egyptologists have said that the builders of the Bent Pyramid suddenly tired of their task and decided to reduce the pyramid's volume, and hence their labour, by

The collapsed pyramid at Meidum

reducing its angle. It has also been said that the bend in the pyramid was predetermined and meant to express a 'double pyramid', that is two pyramids of different angles superimposed, and that this symbolised some unexplained duality. And it has been said that the architect lost his nerve, but one reason for this tantalising possibility — the collapse of the Meidum pyramid at a point when the Bent Pyramid was 70 percent of the way towards completion — has not been countenanced by Egyptologists because it would reintroduce the 'unpalatable conclusion that Snofru did possess three pyramids' (Gardiner). The key word there is possess, for it signals the insistence that pyramids were built for the sole reason of providing a container for the pharaoh's ka, so that Snofru had no business building what he believed at that point to be two perfectly good pyramids.

The Egyptologists' evasions could have gone on indefinitely as long as they could have believed that the pyramid at Meidum had belonged to Snofru's predecessor and had merely crumbled with time. But in *The Riddle of the Pyramids* and the *Journal of Egyptian Archaeology*, Kurt Mendelssohn, professor of physics at Oxford, has argued that Meidum, while nearing completion, came down with a bang as Snofru was already well advanced on his second pyramid—which only then, and for that reason, was continued at a bent angle. (Mendelssohn's opponents in the *JEA* argued well against a single bang, but some initial partial disaster seems likely.)

Overlap in pyramid construction

So why should several pyramids be built in overlapping succession during the reign of a single pharaoh? It is a fact that more large pyramids were built during the IV Dynasty than there were pharaohs to fill them. The answer is in the scale of the task. Herodotus says it took 20 years to build Cheops' Pyramid and 10 years to build the causeway and the earth ramps that served as a kind of scaffolding, with 100,000 men working a three-month shift. Modern calculation of the workforce required does not vary substantially from Herodotus' figure, though it is likely that several thousand men, highly skilled as stone-cutters, masons, surveyors, etc, would have been employed year-round, while the larger requirement for unskilled labour would have been drawn from the fields between July and November, the period of the inundation. All of these people needed training and organisation, as well as feeding, clothing and housing, and the logistics of the operation must have been formidable. It is not the sort of operation that is easily or efficiently mounted at the uncertain occasion of a pharaoh's accession, nor is the size of a pyramid and so the time it will take to build readily geared to the uncertain duration of a pharaoh's reign. The suggestion is rather that pyramid construction was continuous and independent of whether or not there would be enough pharaohs to fill them. And this is what the evidence of Meidum and the Bent Pyramid suggests did happen, the overlap accounted for by the fact that as the first pyramid tapered towards completion, the surplus workforce was immediately engaged on starting a second pyramid.

Pyramids and the state

Whether by intention or as a consequence, this pyramid production line must have had two important effects. The first was that the vast levy of men required would have cut across the division of Upper and Lower Egypt and the parochialism of villages and tribes throughout the length of the valley, the breadth of the Delta. Pyramid building would complete, down to the fibres of society, the unification of the country begun by Menes by force of arms.

The second effect was that whoever was responsible for pyramid building would see their power enhanced. But production of pyramids surplus to the requirements of any one pharaoh, surplus even to the requirements of an entire dynasty, demanded a transcending organising authority. Imhotep's own career suggests the composition of that authority: in part the power of the pharaoh, but also that of the bureaucracy and the priesthood. Pyramids created the apparatus of the state.

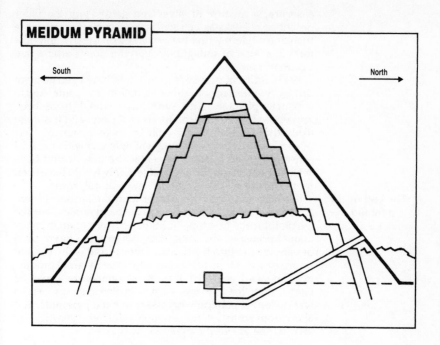

South

North

Symbolism of the Pyramids

There is then the pyramidal form. One can see how constructionally the pyramids began with the mastaba, Zoser's pyramid in fact a stepped mastaba. The achievement in architecture of the pure abstract pyramidal form came, briefly, at Meidum, when before it collapsed its steps were being sheathed in planes. If anything, the disaster was a spur to the technical perfection of the pyramidal symbol. That symbol preceded construction rather than technology dictated symbol seems likely. In Egyptian creation myths there is a primal hill which rises above the waters, and from it ascends the sun. And until the High Dam at Aswan finally put an end to the annual inundation, that was very much the scene in Egypt: villages huddled on mounds to avoid the flood, then its subsidence and the sun drawing from the mud the harvest. This myth is referred to at Medinet Habu and Hermopolis; Heliopolis also claimed **The primal hill** a primal hill, the *benben,* a tapering megalith, a word whose root, *bn,* is bound up with the notion of shining, brilliant, ascending. It is depicted in II Dynasty inscriptions, that is before the pyramid age.

Variations on the pyramidal form continued to be popular throughout Egyptian history, as for example the obelisks whose points or pyramidions were sheathed in electrum, a mixture of silver and gold. Pliny the Elder described obelisks as petrified rays of sunlight, and more than one modern writer has remarked on the pyramid-like form of a burst of sunlight through the clouds after a rare Egyptian rain.

The building of pyramids then would have been no mere drudgery inflicted on the population by some megalomaniac pharaoh. The symbolism would have been appreciated throughout all levels of society, and it is quite likely that far from being built by slave-labour, as Herodotus claims, they were built willingly and with a shared sense of exalted purpose which at the time would have seemed far more important, and certainly would have been more conscious, than creating new political forms.

The end of the pyramid age But here the gods died sooner than the works of men. And those works included not only the pyramids, but the creation for the first time in human history of an organisational principle, the state, that was to serve Egypt until her absorption into the Roman Empire, and is the basis of human organisation to this day. Once the pyramid production line had achieved this, their symbolism could be carried on in lesser forms, such as obelisks; in any case, it was no longer politically necessary to build pyramids, and apart from some inferior examples in later dynasties, by 2500 BC the age of the pyramids was over.

THE GREAT PYRAMIDS OF GIZA

Approaching the Pyramids

Half a day should be allowed for the visit to the Giza Pyramids, though you should return again at night. They are approached along a broad straight road, originally built for that same Empress Eugénie who attended the opening night at the Opera House, so that she could cover the 11 km from Cairo in her carriage. This Sharia al-Ahram or Road of the Pyramids once passed across fellahin's fields which would flood with the rising of the Nile, but nowadays the entire route has been built up. There is therefore, at first, something ordinary about the approach, as though you were off to a funfair on the edge of town, expecting at any moment the distant screams of roller coaster passengers as they plunged down papier-maché mountains.

But even the Pyramids themselves initially conspire to deflate anticipation. One of the savants accompanying Napoleon described his approach: 'Seen from a distance they produce the same kind of effect as do high mountain peaks. The nearer one approaches, the more this effect decreases. Only when at last you are within a short distance of these regular masses is a wholly different impression produced; you are struck by surprise, and as soon as you have reached the top of the slope, your ideas change in a flash. Finally, when you have reached the foot of the Great Pyramid, you are seized with a vivid and powerful

The Sphinx and Chephren's Pyramid

emotion, tempered by a sort of stupefaction, almost overwhelming in its effects.'

Even so, you might just as easily be overwhelmed by touts urging you to ride their donkey, horse or camel, and by numberless 'guides' and 'watchmen' who gather about you like mosquitoes, endlessly trying to lure you into ruined little temples with the promise of an undiscovered mummy or reliefs of pharaonic pornography. In the old days, visitors would come with a dragoman who wielded a big stick for which you are bound to develop the greatest nostalgia. Mark Twain, who led a party of tourists here in the 1860s, attempted escape by climbing to the top of Cheops' Pyramid but was pursued by an Arab whom he offered $1 if he could race to the top of Chephren's Pyramid and back to the top of Cheops' within nine minutes, in the hope that the man would break his neck. Three dollars later an exasperated Twain, now joined by the man's mother, offered them each $100 if they would jump off the Pyramid head first.

The best times to visit the Pyramids are at dawn, at sunset and at night when they form as much a part of the natural order as the sun, the moon and the stars. Flaubert recalled the view from the top of Cheops' Pyramid: 'The sun was rising just opposite; the whole valley of the Nile, bathed in mist, seemed to be a still white sea; and the desert behind us, with its hillocks of sand, another ocean, deep purple, its waves all petrified'. My first visit was at night. I had gone to the son et lumiere, the Arabic programme, so that I would not have to listen to any of the usual tourist drivel, but could instead enjoy the play of lights to the eerie accompaniment of this booming, gutteral but poetic language. The programme over but some floodlights on, I walked up past the Sphinx and stood between the Pyramids of Cheops and Chephren. And then suddenly the lights went out. Black night. The great stones rising on either side, picked out by the moon and stars. The feeling, as Napoleon said here to his army, of 'forty centuries of history looking down upon us', feeling it in the most awesome way.

Statistics   The road arrives at the Mena House Hotel and then curves sharply to the left, mounting a gentle slope and finishing at the north end of the plateau, almost directly opposite the Great Pyramid, that of Cheops. This is the oldest of the group and the largest, and the others, Chephren and Mycerinus, stand in descending order of age and size along a southwest axis, each identically oriented 8.5° west of magnetic north; when built they were probably aligned precisely with the North Star, their entrance corridors aiming straight at it. At first the second pyramid, that of Chephren, seems largest, but that is because it

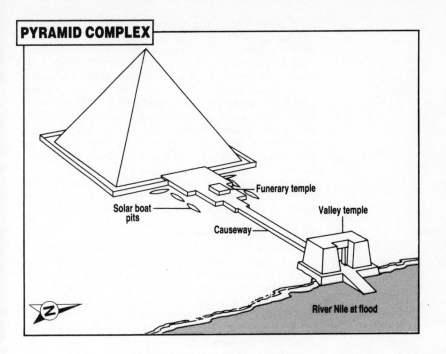

Funerary temple

Solar boat
pits

Valley temple

Causeway

River Nile at flood

stands on higher ground and retains its casing towards its peak. Its present height is 136.4 metres (originally 143 metres) and its volume is 2,200,000 cubic metres; this compares with a height of 137.2 metres (originally 146.6 metres) for the Great Pyramid of Cheops, which has a volume of 2,550,000 cubic metres. This pyramid was built of over 2,500,000 enormous blocks of limestone cut from the Moqattam and locally, though about 170,000 have been removed by Arabs and Turks since the founding of Cairo. Mycerinus is much smaller, rising only to a height of 65.5 metres, though it is still imposing, and it contributes to the satisfying arrangement of the group. Napoleon astonished his officers with the calculation that the stones from these three pyramids would be sufficient to build a wall 3 metres high and 0.3 metres thick around the whole of France.

But the Pyramids do not have this rocky ledge entirely to themselves. There are smaller attendant pyramids, some at least for royal wives, and suburban rows of mastabas for nobles and princes of the blood. There are the remains of temples and causeways; there are solar boat pits; and there is the Sphinx. A pyramid was never merely a self-sufficient geometrically shaped tumulus of masonry raised above a royal burial; it was the culminating point of a vast funerary area comprising, apart from the pyramid

**A pyramid
complex**

111

itself, three parts. First, near the desert edge and over-looking the cultivation so as to be accessible by boat in the inundation season was a modest *valley chapel*. From it led a walled-in *causeway*, as long as 500 metres, upwards to the *funerary temple* proper, this abutting on to the east side of the pyramid, where a false door permitted the deceased pharaoh to emerge in order to partake of the offered feasts. Also, on several sides of a pyramid, set in pits, *wooden boats* have been found. Whether these were only symbolic or actually used is not known; some have supposed they enabled the pharaoh to follow the sun god across the skies, but as they have been found facing all four points of the compass they could as easily have been intended to enable the pharaoh to go wherever he desired. For convenience, however, they will be referred to here as solar boats.

The Pyramid of Cheops

Climbing the Great Pyramid

The polished casing to the **Pyramid of Cheops** (Khufu) is entirely gone and so you are presented with the tiered courses of limestone blocks, an invitation to climb to the platform at the top, 10 metres square. This used to be a fairly easy and entirely safe thing to do, as guides would simply haul you up, one at each arm, a third shoving from below. Climbing the Pyramids is now technically forbidden, however, which leaves the field open to the more adventurous or the more foolhardy to make the attempt unassisted. The ascent is best made at the northeast corner, each 'step' a metre-high block, and will take 15 to 20 minutes. The footing is more difficult on the way down; also you are more prone to tiredness and vertigo (you must now look *down*). Recently a young man who slept on top while awaiting the dawn fell out of bed, so to speak. There is no stopping a fall; he bounced only twice before obliteration.

Going inside

The squeamish might content themselves with going inside. Here the only thing to fear is fear itself, in the form of claustrophobia and difficulty for some in breathing due to inadequate oxygen, and also the possibility that you might get locked in, which in fact happened one night to my brother (more on the very real dangers of being sealed up, temporarily and even permanently, in ancient tombs when you read about Saqqara).

The descending corridor

You *enter at the north face* through an opening made by Caliph al-Mamun in his search for treasure (though it is probable that this pyramid had been robbed as early as the First Intermediate Period), and soon come to the *original corridor* which descends for 100 metres to a depth of 30 metres beneath the surface of the bedrock. It reaches an *unfinished chamber* of no interest, and as this corridor is constricted (1.3 metres high, one metre wide) and

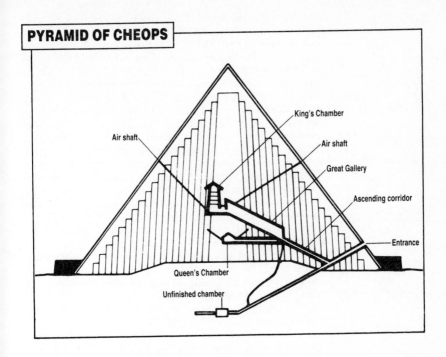

PYRAMID OF CHEOPS

King's Chamber

Air shaft

Air shaft

Great Gallery

Ascending corridor

Entrance

Queen's Chamber

Unfinished chamber

slippery, it is not usually open to the public. Why this lowest chamber was never finished is not known; Herodotus said it was subject to flooding by the Nile.

The ascending corridor
Instead, about 20 metres from the entrance along the descending corridor you come to a block of granite designed to prevent access to the *ascending corridor*, though al-Mamun merely hollowed out the rock to the left and you soon find yourself crouching your way upwards (height again 1.3 metres, width one metre) for 40 metres. The gradient is 1 in 2, and so can be quite tiring, but arrival at the Great Gallery at least permits a stretch. Here there is a *shaft* (right) which winds down to the descending corridor—purpose unknown. There is also a *horizontal corridor*, again only 1.3 metres high for most of its length,

The Queen's Chamber and Great Gallery
which leads to the so-called *Queen's Chamber*, nearly square with a pointed roof of gigantic blocks. But best by far is the ascending *Great Gallery*, 8.5 metres high, 47 metres long, a marvel of precision masonry, of which it has been said that neither a needle nor a hair can be inserted into the joints of the stones.

The King's Chamber
This gives on to the principal tomb chamber, commonly called the *King's Chamber*, 42.5 metres above the surface of

113

the bedrock, 5.22 metres wide and 10.44 metres long, that is a double square, aligned east-west. On the north and south walls, a metre above the floor, are the rectangular mouths of the two *ventilation shafts* which extend to the surfaces of the pyramid. The chamber is built entirely in pink Aswan granite and roofed over with nine huge granite slabs laid horizontally, and above these (seen by means of a ladder leading to a passage in the upper south wall of the Great Gallery) are four more granite layers, each separated by a *relieving chamber*, possibly meant to distribute the full weight of the pyramid away from the King's Chamber, though in fact this job is accomplished by the topmost pointed roof of limestone blocks. It was in these relieving chambers that the only inscriptions in any of the Giza Pyramids were found—the cartouche, traced several times in red, of Khufu, Cheops. His mummy, if it found its way to this pyramid at all, would have been placed in this King's Chamber; the sarcophagus is empty.

It is here that you might think about the great weight upon you. Over your head is 95 metres of solid pyramid, more than enough to squash you very thin for a very long time. Unlike the Meidum pyramid, however, the Pyramid of Cheops has been shown by Swiss engineer H. Roessler (1952) to be exceptionally stable. The building blocks are far larger than those used for earlier pyramids and they are precisely fitted together, while the casing blocks overlaying the basic step structure rest upon foundations slotted into the bedrock. The weight of the pyramid itself contributes to its stability, but not simply its dead weight; the stepped inclined buttresses throw much of this weight towards the centre. At every level the pyramid's horizontal thrusts are directed towards the central core, while 35 percent of the vertical thrusts are transmitted to the inner core (that is the line running from the top of the pyramid *through you* to the base), only the remaining thrusts being carried down into the bedrock. In fact the bigger the pyramid the more stable it becomes.

Coming out of the pyramid you can see on the north side, also on the east, the remains of the original *enclosure wall*, about 10 metres from the base. Backing against this wall on the east side is the basalt paving of **Cheops' funerary temple**, about all that remains of it, and only occasional traces too of the *causeway* that would have come up from the valley temple. The **three small pyramids**, from 15 to 20 metres high, probably belonged to Cheops' queens or sisters.

Solar boat museum   Three empty boat pits have been found near Cheops' Pyramid, but in 1954 a fourth pit revealed a dismantled **solar boat** of Syrian cedar. This magnificent craft has been reassembled and housed in its own specially-constructed

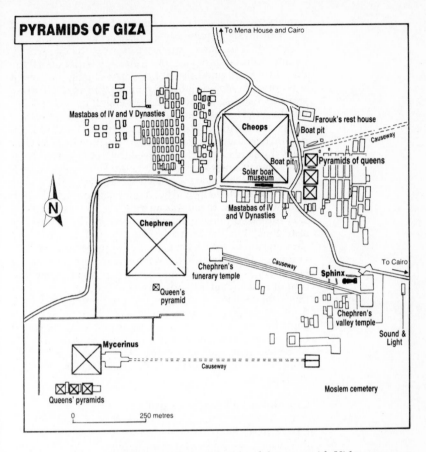

To Mena House and Cairo

Mastabas of IV and V Dynasties

Cheops

Farouk's rest house

Boat pit

Causeway

Boat pit

Solar boat museum

Pyramids of queens

Chephren

Mastabas of IV and V Dynasties

Queen's pyramid

Chephren's funerary temple

Causeway

Sphinx

To Cairo

Chephren's valley temple

Sound & Light

Mycerinus

Causeway

Moslem cemetery

Queens' pyramids

N

0   250 metres

museum on the south side of the pyramid. Video cameras
lowered through drill holes into a fifth pit in 1987 discovered another boat perfectly preserved in 4600-year old
air beneath the hermetic seal of 1.5-metre thick limestone
slabs.

The Sphinx

An outcrop of hard grey and soft yellow limestone, useless
as building material, was left standing in the quarry from
which Cheops cut many of the blocks for his pyramid. His
son Chephren had the happy idea of shaping it into a
figure—lion's body, god's face, though perhaps Chephren's own, and wearing the royal headdress with
uraeus. The Egyptians would have regarded it as a symbol
of strength and wisdom combined, but the Greeks applied
their word sphinx to it, recalling a lion's body but the
breasts and head of a woman given to putting riddles to

115

passers-by, and so this most famous **Sphinx** has acquired an air of mystery quite foreign to its intention.

Nevertheless, some mysteries are associated with it. Neither Herodotus nor any other classical writer until Pliny the Elder mentioned the Sphinx, presumably because it was buried in sand. Prints and photographs of recent times show its features looming from an engulfing sea of sand, but this is all too assiduously cleared today, some mystery swept away with it. The future Tuthmosis IV (XVIII Dyn) dreamt here that if he was to become pharaoh he must clear away the sands: his stelae between the Sphinx' paws commemorate this first known restoration. During the Turkish domination the Sphinx was used for target practice and its nose, which originally had been cemented on, fell off; 18th C drawings show that it was missing long before Napoleon was supposed to have done the damage. The uraeus has also gone, but the beard is being pieced together and should soon be struck back on. In the son et lumiere programmes, the Sphinx is given the role of narrator which it performs, as I have said, much better in Arabic when you cannot understand a word. This is in fact one of the best times for viewing it or, after the programme, having a drink on the terrace of the Pavilion of Cheops, for then it gains in perspective against the more distant Pyramids. It may not otherwise seem as large as you had imagined: it is 20 metres high and 48.5 metres long, much of its bulk crouched within the quarry so that only its head overtops the horizon.

Chephren's Pyramid Complex

Immediately in front of the Sphinx and associated with it is a IV Dynasty temple, one reason for believing the face on the Sphinx is a god's and not Chephren's, for the Egyptians did not build temples to their kings. Adjacent and to the south is **Chephren's Valley Temple**, facing east. This is the only IV Dynasty sanctuary to retain its grandeur, its exceptional state of preservation owing to having been buried in the sands and not discovered until 1853 by Mariette. The material is pink Aswan granite, majestically and simply assembled in strong verticals and horizontals, square monolithic pillars supporting massive granite architraves. It was here that Mariette discovered the magnificent diorite statue of Chephren (Room 42, Ground Floor, Egyptian Museum). The purpose of this temple is uncertain, or rather certain for some and contradicted by others. One view is that valley temples were used for mummification; others think the site too exposed and that embalming would have been done either at the pharaoh's Memphis palace or at the base of the pyramid, in the funerary temple. There is at least more general agreement that here was performed the 'Opening of the Mouth' ceremony at which the ka entered the deceased's body. The ka always required a secure residence, hence pyramids and immutable bodies, though it would also inhabit the mortuary statue of the pharaoh, such as that one in the Egyptian Museum, one of 23 that sat round the main T-shaped chamber.

You should now follow if you can the traces of Chephren's *causeway* up to his **Funerary Temple** at the base of his pyramid. More of this temple survives than of Cheops', the walls formed of possibly the largest blocks ever used in building, one of them 13.4 metres long and weighing 163,000 kilos. To the south of the pyramid is a ruined small pyramid, probably of a queen.

The **Pyramid of Chephren** (Khafre) compares to Cheops' in size, seemingly exceeds it in height and is also capped with its original casing. But its interior is less interesting, while the outside ascent is much more difficult, requiring an hour to get to the casing, progress being very dangerous thence upwards because the smooth surface offers no hold. One of the earlier explorers and snatchers of antiquities was Belzoni, born in Italy but first achieving fame for his 'human pyramid' act on the stage of the Sadlers Wells in London. He was the first European to enter this pyramid (1818) and promptly emblazoned his name on the south wall of the burial chamber. When Flaubert entered the chamber 33 years later he recorded: 'Under Belzoni's name, and no less large, is that of a M Just de Chasseloup-Laubat. One is irritated by the number of imbeciles' names written everywhere: on the top of the Great Pyramid there is a certain Buffard, 79 Rue Saint-Martin, wallpaper manufacturer, in black letters; an English fan of Jenny Lind's has written her name; there is also a pear, representing Louis-Phillipe'.

When the Egyptians built their pyramids it was with a feeling for the sublime power of the plane, without reliefs, inscriptions or any detailing whatsoever. Once the polished limestone casings were set in place, the pyramids both literally and symbolically repulsed the touch of mortals — well, that was the idea, anyway. One of the high points of a visit to the Pyramids in Roman times was the spectacle of men from a nearby village shinning up from the ground to their very tips; while one Roman woman scribbled on a casing stone, 'I saw the Pyramids without you; sadly I shed tears here', a lament copied down by a 15th C pilgrim, when the casing was more extensive than now.

Last of the Great Pyramids
The **Pyramid of Mycerinus** (Menkaure) has only one-tenth of the volume of the other two pyramids and effectively

marks the end of the pyramid age. The last pharaoh of the IV Dynasty built a quite different sort of tomb at Saqqara, while the pyramids of the next dynasty were small and shoddy. Though last of the great pyramids, Mycerinus' was built well, with granite used for the lower courses and a casing that remained intact until the 16th C. An attempt was made by the caliph in 1215 to destroy all the Pyramids and his workmen started with Mycerinus'. After eight months they gave up. 'Considering the vast masses that have been taken away, it might be supposed that the building would have been completely destroyed, but so immense is the pile that the stones are scarcely missed. Only on one of its sides can be noticed any trace of the impression which it was attempted to be made', wrote the historian Abd el Latif. Though you can enter, the interior is not interesting. Opposite the south face are three small pyramids, while against the east are the remains of Mycerinus' funerary temple.

Mons Venus   Herodotus recorded a belief in Greece that this pyramid was in fact built by Rhodopis, a beautiful courtesan from Thrace who flourished in Egypt, charging a building stone for her services. The Pyramid of Mycerinus is built of at least 200,000 granite and limestone blocks. But it is not only for that reason that the story is untrue.

PRACTICAL INFORMATION

The *Practical Information* section at the end of the *Cairo: Mother of the World* chapter contains information on getting to the Pyramids and on the Sound and Light show. One of the most agreeable things you can do while out here is to have tea or a meal at the Mena House.

Although you can have a general view of the Pyramids and Sphinx at any time of day or night, **access** to the Sphinx, tombs and valley temples, and **entry** into the chambers of the Pyramids is from 8am to 4.30pm daily. The only fees are for seeing the solar boat in its glass-enclosed chamber (LE6, students with card LE2.50 — open 9am to 2pm daily, closed Tuesdays) and for entering the Pyramids (LE5, students with card LE2); tickets for the Pyramids should be bought at the kiosk at the top of the road coming up from the Mena House Hotel towards the north side of the Pyramid of

Cheops. Con men may attempt to extort money from you for simply staring at the monuments, while others will press their services upon you as guides or try to sell you fake antiquities and other rubbish. All are to be ignored, and if necessary the Tourist Police invoked. You should accept assistance and agree a price only if you want help in climbing the Pyramids.

You can **ride on horseback or camel-back** across the desert from the Pyramids to **Saqqara**. The journey will take at least 3 hours in each direction, and spending just a little time at Saqqara means an 8-hour expedition in all. For this reason you should resist offers of hire by the hour and negotiate a price for the entire day. Camels will cost about LE25 and can carry two people, though that is not advisable; horses cost a bit less. There is some dispute as to which animal is better; most people prefer horses over longer distances. Either way, all but the most hardened rider can expect to end the day feeling pretty sore.

There are **Sound and Light** shows nightly at 7.30 and 8.30pm. English programmes are at 7.30 on Mondays, Wednesdays, Fridays and Saturdays, and at 8.30 on Thursday. Admission LE6 except for the Arabic programme which is LE1. Seating is on a terrace facing the valley temple of the Pyramid of Chephren, ie by the Sphinx. Bring a sweater; it can get cool on the edge of the desert, even in summer.

Almost any taxi driver will know what you mean if you say Sound and Light. Agree a per-hour or all-in rate if you want him to wait (thus avoiding any difficulty in getting a ride back, though you can walk over to the Mena House and get a taxi there); the hotel limousines have a set rate for this. Also there are buses, but these will take you to the Mena House Hotel and you will have to walk back down the Pyramids Road till you reach the Sound and Light sign (on the right as you face Cairo) and then walk to the right, through the village on the edge of the desert escarpment. Or if you are alert you can alight at the sign (it is about 1000 metres before the Mena House Hotel), saving yourself some shoe leather. Another alternative is to take a tour, which will include admission and the ride out and back. This works out at about as much as it would cost one person to take a taxi and keep it waiting; for 2 or more people it is better to take the taxi.

MEMPHIS AND SAQQARA

Saqqara is 32 km by road from Cairo and 21 km south of the Giza Pyramids. The necropolis extends about 7 km north to south along the desert plateau and looks down over the palm groves that cover the site of **Memphis**, about 6 km to the southeast in the valley of the Nile. Memphis was the capital of the Old Kingdom, its palaces and shrines of that period built of mud brick for the span of the living and now vanished; Saqqara, built of stone to endure eternity, survives.

The Saqqara road is a left turn off the Road to the Pyramids at the traffic lights immediately after a canal about 1500 metres before the Mena House Hotel. It is a pleasant country road with glimpses to the right of the Libyan Desert and the V Dynasty pyramids of Abusir. (You can also ride across the desert by camel or horse from the Giza Pyramids in about three hours). You come first to the turning, on your right, for Saqqara; or you can carry straight on for the left-hand turning to the Memphis site. Alternatively, you can take the bus from the Giza Pyramids to Badrashein and can ask to be let off at Memphis. It is best to visit Saqqara early in the morning to avoid the heat, and so to call on Memphis afterwards. But for context, Memphis will be mentioned first.

Old Kingdom Capital

History of Memphis
Memphis probably began as a fortress by which Menes controlled the land and water routes between Upper and Lower Egypt and kept the conquered inhabitants of the Delta in subjection. By the III Dynasty it must have become a sizeable capital, as the Saqqara necropolis suggests, but it may not have been fixed. The IV Dynasty pharaohs built their pyramids to the north at Giza and might well have had their palaces near there too. One can imagine Memphis developing in stages like Arab Fustat and its successors, decamping northwards. Whether it was the Mediterranean breezes that attracted, or the growing dominance of the sun cult at Heliopolis, so closely associated with pyramid development, is not known. By the VI Dynasty, however, the old site of Memphis had been reoccupied, its attraction the venerable sanctuary of Ptah. From the court of Pepi and its associated monuments came the name *Men-nefru-Mire*, The Beauty of King Mire (Pepi), later abbreviated to Menfe, in Greek Memphis.

Although no longer capital, in the New Kingdom Memphis rivalled Thebes in grandeur, embellished in particular by Ramses II's mania for building. During the 5th C BC when the Persians ruled Egypt from here and

Herodotus visited the city, it was a great cosmopolitan centre, a foreshadowing of Alexandria, with many Greeks and Jews, Phoenicians and Libyans amongst its population, as full of Oriental spectacle as Cairo is today. Herodotus, in his hydrology of Egypt, which fascinated him, wrote that 'when the Nile overflows, the whole country is converted into a sea, and the towns, which alone remain above water, look like islands in the Aegean. At these times water transport is used all over the country, instead of merely along the course of the river and anyone going from Naucratis to Memphis would pass right by the Pyramids ... The priests told me that it was Menes, the first king of Egypt, who raised the dam which protects Memphis from the floods ... On the land which had been drained by the diversion of the river, King Menes built his city and afterwards on the north and west sides of the town excavated a lake, communicating with the river.' As late as the 12th C, Abd el Latif could write that 'the ruins still offer, to those who contemplate them, a collection of such marvellous beauty that the intelligence is confounded, and the most eloquent man would be unable to describe them adequately'. But towards the end of the Mameluke period the dikes around Memphis fell into disrepair and at every inundation the level of the ground was raised.

Memphis today Today the centuries of Nile mud have swallowed Memphis entirely, so much so that it is impossible to stand here and soliloquise on how the once mighty has fallen — there is, simply, so little to stir reflection. And even had the dikes been maintained, the more ancient stratas of Memphis would have been lost. Herodotus exactly describes those conditions, persisting until the building of the High Dam at Aswan, which annually drowned the valley and the Delta and gradually covered the past with mud, so that settlements built upon themselves, one strata upon another, to form what in Arabic are known as *tells*. The earliest mud brick houses, palaces and sanctuaries have long since disintegrated beneath the wash of the annual flood, explaining why so much is known of the Egyptian dead, who dwelt in stone on high desert ground, while so little is known of the living.

At Memphis there is a modern building erected for the sole purpose of roofing over a supine **colossus of Ramses II**, brother to the one outside the Cairo railway station. This Ramses is the victim of monumental indifference: the Egyptian government gave him to the British Museum — which failed to collect. He lies here with his right fist clenched, like a cataleptic Gulliver, bound down by brain seizure rather than ropes. Several smaller statues stand or lie in the grass beneath palms near the covered colossus. Otherwise the immediate area has been turned into a garden, and set up along the central pathway like a plaster gnome is a friendly alabaster **sphinx** dating from the New Kingdom. If you walk a bit beyond this, no more than 100 metres eastwards, you can survey the shapeless mounds that cloak the ancient city. The faint remains of the vast **Temple of Ptah** lie waterlogged beside the village of Mit Rahinah. Or from the garden with its sphinx follow the road to Saqqara for 100 metres; off its north side are the alabaster **mummification beds** where the Apis bulls (see the Serapeum at Saqqara) were prepared for burial.

The Egypt Exploration Society is now excavating at Memphis; perhaps in a decade or so there will be more to see.

Saqqara

Touring the necropolis The Saqqara site has a far more desert feel than Giza; the sands wash about your feet nearly everywhere. Also it is dotted with untended holes left by excavators, some of terrific depth and not always enclosed. It would be dangerous for children on the loose, and adults should mind their step. Many tombs, once discovered and examined, have been closed again and some even sanded over. The most comfortable way to explore the site is to go first to Zoser's funerary complex, visiting also the Pyramid of Unas nearby, and then to drive round to the refreshment tent (or walk across the sands to it) from where you can visit the Mastaba of Akhti-hotep and Ptah-hotep, the Mastaba of Ti and the Serapeum.

Saqqara, from Sokkar, the Memphite god of the dead, was a necropolis from the unification of Egypt through the Ptolemaic period, and it is the site also of a Coptic monastery destroyed by the Arabs c.960, so that discoveries here span 4000 years. In historical range and the quantity and value of what has been found here — monuments, works of art, texts and vases — there can be few archaeological sites in all the world, let alone Egypt, to compare with Saqqara. Even so, serious examination of the site only began in the mid-19th C and what remains to be discovered is incalculable. Early in 1986 there was the most important find since Howard Carter broke into Tutankhamun's tomb; the discovery here of the tomb of Maya, a close friend of the famous boy-pharaoh. (It will not be open to the public for several years.)

Discovery Except for Zoser's Step Pyramid, Saqqara was ignored, its revelations unsuspected, until 1851 when Auguste Mariette discovered the Serapeum. Even the funerary complex immediately surrounding the Step Pyramid went undiscovered until 1924, and its restoration, to which Jean-Phillipe Lauer has given a lifetime, continues to this day. Cecil M Firth's campaign of 1924–7 overturned accepted notions

The world's first building in stone: the Step Pyramid at Saqqara

about the origins of Egyptian architecture in stone which, because of the gigantic blocks used at Giza, was thought to have developed from megalithic monuments. Instead, at Zoser's complex, one sees a stone architecture which replicates the use of brick in its size and courses, and which also is full of imitative references to rush matting, reed and wood forms. One of the greatest achievements of Egyptian civilisation was to sever stone from the rock and to make of it a building material unsurpassed to this day. It happened here, for the first time, at Saqqara, with some hesitancy in the new technology but astonishing artistic brilliance.

Zoser's Funerary Complex

Zoser's funerary complex, dominated by the Step Pyramid, is 544 metres from north to south, 277 metres from east to west, and entirely surrounded by a magnificent panelled and bastioned **enclosure wall** of fine limestone. It still survives to a height of 3.7 metres at some places along its south side, while on the east side, near the southeast corner, it has been rebuilt with stones found in the sand to its original height of 10.48 metres. This vast white wall in itself, once easily visible from Memphis, must have conferred enormous prestige on Zoser and his architect Imhotep. Lauer was himself at first an architect and was called in by Firth when it was realised that the complex could be accurately reconstructed using the original stones.

123

Though there are many *false doors* in the enclosure wall for the ka to come and go, there is only one *entrance* (1) for the living, at the southeast corner. The narrow passage is through a fortress-like tower and gives on to a vestibule where you can see on either side the leaves of a *simulated double door* thrown open, complete with hinge pins and sockets. Ahead of you is a *colonnaded corridor* (2), its columns engaged and ribbed in imitation of palm stems (the protective ceiling is modern concrete). At the far end is a broad *hypostyle hall* (3) with four pairs of engaged columns, and on your right as you enter the court a half open ka door. This is where the statue base bearing Imhotep's titles was found. Before leaving the hall, notice that the columns are comprised of drums seldom exceeding 25 cm in height, one of many details of the masonry which betray Imhotep's hesitancy in working with this new material, stone.

You now emerge into the **Great South Court** (4), and along the wall to your left is a section of rebuilt wall with a *frieze of cobras* (5). The cobra, *uraeus* in Latin, was an emblem of royalty and an instrument of protection, always appearing on the pharaoh's headdress and able to destroy his enemies by breathing flames. The cobra was worshipped in Lower Egypt, and so here in this early dynasty it also emphasises Zoser's mastery over the conquered peoples of the Delta. Near here is a shaft leading to Zoser's *southern tomb* (6), similar in its faience decoration to that beneath the Step Pyramid. There is a relief here of Zoser running the Heb-Sed race (see below). One explanation for two tombs is that early pharaohs thereby demonstrated their connection with the two Egypts, so a southern and northern tomb. Possibly the canopic jars containing Zoser's viscera were placed here, the body beneath the pyramid (where in fact a foot was found).

Zoser's Step Pyramid

The **Step Pyramid** (7) and its place in the development of pyramid building has already been referred to in an earlier chapter. Now you have a first-hand opportunity to examine its features. Despite its 62-metre height, it was built of fairly small limestone blocks, far smaller than those enormous blocks at Giza. Though working with stone, Imhotep was still thinking in terms of mud brick. But even in the enlargement of his monument from mastaba to pyramid you can detect signs of Imhotep's growing confidence in the new medium: at the southeast corner where the casing has come away you can see the smaller stonework of the *mastaba,* as you can if you walk along the east face of the pyramid. Also note how regularly the courses are laid, both of the mastaba and the pyramid as a whole, and how well shaped and fitted the stones are. In technique, Imhotep was without fault. The last enlarged

FUNERARY COMPLEX OF ZOSER

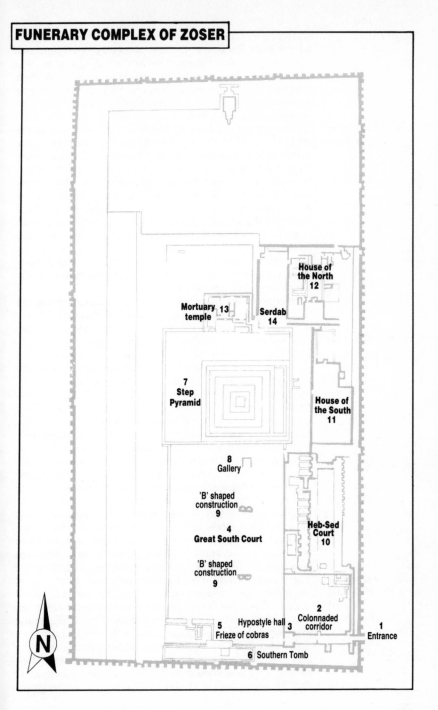

House of the North 12

Mortuary temple 13

Serdab 14

7 Step Pyramid

House of the South 11

8 Gallery

'B' shaped construction 9

4 Great South Court

'B' shaped construction 9

Heb-Sed Court 10

5 Frieze of cobras

Hypostyle hall 3

2 Colonnaded corridor

1 Entrance

6 Southern Tomb

N

mastaba measured 63 metres each way and a little over 8 metres high. Recall that the first pyramid erected over this mastaba rose four steps; the further pyramid of two additional steps increased the total volume by more than four fold. The entire monument was then sheathed in fine limestone from Tura, just to the south of modern Cairo, as were the Giza Pyramids.

Entrance to the pyramid

The original entrance to the Step Pyramid was at the north face, but in the XXVI Dynasty, known as the Saite period for its dynasty's origins at Sais in the Delta, a *gallery* (8) was dug from the Great South Court to the chambers beneath the pyramid. Permission and keys will have to be asked for at the office of the Inspector of Antiquities to the northeast of the Pyramid of Teti. The Saites admired the works of the Old Kingdom and it is quite possible they tunnelled their way into the pyramid out of sheer archaeological curiosity. After 60 metres you come to the main central shaft from where there are impressive views up into the pyramid and down towards the *burial chamber* which is sealed with a huge granite plug.

Emerging once again into the Great South Court, you see two *B-shaped constructions* (9) near the centre. These marked the limits of Upper and Lower Egypt, the gap between them symbolically spanned by Zoser in the Heb-Sed race. (A *relief* in the southern tomb shows Zoser in full stride, the two B-shaped constructions to the rear and fore.) The Heb-Sed race was one of the ceremonies during the five-day jubilee which occurred in the thirtieth year — that is at the interval of one generation — of the pharaoh's reign. It is possible that at some earlier period, power was granted only for 30 years, the chieftain then deposed, perhaps killed, to spare the land from decline because of his failing strength. This jubilee, therefore, was a renewal of the vital forces of the pharaoh and his ka, and so of all Egypt.

The Heb-Sed race

Also at his jubilee the pharaoh re-enacted his coronation, sitting first on the throne of Upper Egypt, then on the throne of Lower Egypt, each time presenting gifts to the various priesthoods before they returned to their provinces. Participation in the festival obliged the priests to recognise the supremacy of the pharaoh over their own local deities. These ceremonies, however, including the ritual race, would not have taken place here but at Memphis. The funerary complex was meant as a cosmic 'stand-in' for the actual jubilee site — it perpetuated the regenerating Heb-Sed in eternal stone. This explains the extraordinary film set quality of the Heb-Sed Court.

Significance of the Heb-Sed Court

The **Heb-Sed Court** (10) in the southeast part of the complex is rectangular and flanked to east and west by *shrines*, each one representing a province. They are hardly more than facades, as in a Hollywood Western. Access to the offering niches is by circumventing a screen wall, disguising the lack of depth, for the tall buildings are mere dummies, filled with rubble. Half open doors with hinges, imitations of the wooden originals, receive immortality in stone. In actuality, these shrines would have been tents with wooden poles and cross-supports. The chapels are not uniform; some have a curved cornice, as though the underlying frame represented flexed wood; other roofs are horizontal with the outward curve of the cavetto cornice that was to become so familiar a feature of Egyptian architecture, and torus moulding. Drawing on earlier building materials, Imhotep here invented the language of stone architecture. Cornices, torus mouldings, stone corner posts and columns and a variety of capitals appear for the first time in history at Saqqara. All the more astonishing that the effect is so delicate and beautifully proportioned.

A stone *platform* at the south end of the court is probably where the two thrones of Egypt stood for the re-enactment of the coronation, while at the north end of the court, to the left, is a *base with four pairs of feet*, most likely those of statues of Zoser, his wife and two daughters.

North of the Heb-Sed Court is another spacious court and the **House of the South** (11) with engaged proto-Doric columns. These Doric-style columns were never popular in Egypt where planes and hence smoothly-rounded columns were preferred to the Aegean play of light and shadow. There is the peculiarity of the door being placed asymmetrically, owing to the prototype facade being no more than a curtain, the door therefore needing to abut a column for support. As with the shrines in the Heb-Sed Court, the House of the South and the House of the North would actually have had wooden frames. They may have been sanctuaries, or possibly they represent government buildings of Upper and Lower Egypt.

First tourist graffiti Inside the corridor are the first known examples of tourist graffiti, written in a cursive form of hieroglyphics and dating from the New Kingdom. The visitors, scribes from Thebes, express their admiration for Zoser's achievement, though here and elsewhere some settle for the ancient equivalent of 'Kilroy was here', while one smug crackpot, taking exception to some illiterate graffiti he must have seen, scribbled: 'The scribe of clever fingers came, a clever scribe without his equal among any men of Memphis, the scribe Amenemhet. I say: Explain to me these words. My heart is sick when I see the work of their hands. It is like the work of a woman who has no mind.'

The **House of the North** (12) is similar to that of the South except here the columns have the form of a papyrus plant, the shaft the triangular stem, the capital the fanning head.

The **mortuary temple** (13) at the north face of the

pyramid is largely in ruins. The original entrance to the burial chamber beneath the pyramid led from this temple. To the east of the temple is the **serdab** (14), as startling now as it was to Firth when he uncovered it. It is a masonry box, tilted slightly back and with two small holes drilled through its north face. A window at the side, put there by the excavators, allows you to peer in. And there is Zoser! A life-size painted *limestone statue* as you realise after the initial surprise, but for all the world like a strapped-in astronaut in his space capsule, his eyes fixed through the holes on the North Star, awaiting blast-off and immortality. The circumpolar stars and the North Star itself were 'those that know no destruction' or 'those that know no weariness', for they never set and so never died; this was the place of eternal blessedness for which Egyptians longed. And there is Zoser. It is absolutely convincing. It is this which impresses about the ancient Egyptians again and again, how they gave as well as they could mechanical effect to their illusions. They put California body-freezers to shame. Alas for poor Zoser, the unbelieving Mr Firth removed the original statue to the Antiquities Museum in Cairo; this is a copy. But then again, the substitution probably does not bother Zoser's ka, and it lives here still, and at dark of night it rockets starwards and mingles with the universe.

Pharaonic astronaut

The Pyramid of Unas

Unas was the last pharaoh of the V Dynasty. About 350 years mark the distance between Zoser's Step Pyramid, the Great Pyramids at Giza, and this heap of rubble that is Unas' pyramid. These monuments graphically portray the rise and decline of the Old Kingdom sun cult.

The Pyramid of Unas was approached by a kilometre-long *causeway*, part of which has been reconstructed, including a very short section of its walls and roof, for it was entirely enclosed. A slit in the roof allowed the sunlight to illuminate the inscribed walls which were lively with everyday scenes. On the north side several *mastabas* are arranged like village houses on either side of narrow lanes. The best is of Princess Idut (V Dyn) with ten rooms. On the south side of the causeway there are impressive *boat pits*. Also, about 150 metres to the south are the sanded over ruins of the **Monastery of St Jeremias**, founded in the second half of the 5th C and destroyed by the Arabs around 960. Practically all of its paintings and carvings have been removed to the Coptic Museum in Old Cairo.

The **Pyramid of Unas** looks like a pile of dirt, certainly when approached from the east. On the west side its stones are more evident, but are disarrayed. Even originally it rose only about 18.5 metres; its core was loose blocks

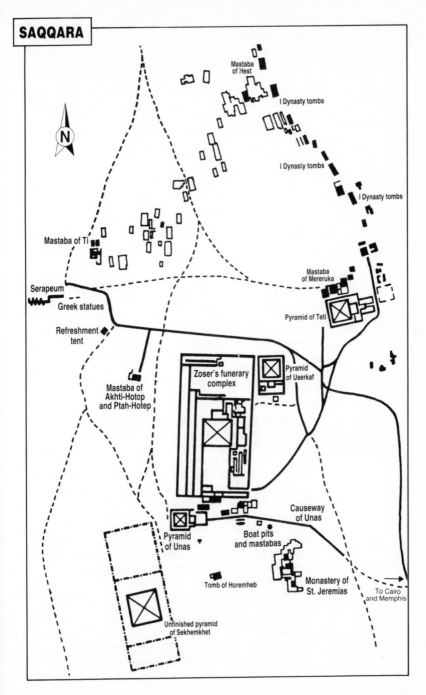

SAQQARA

N

Mastaba of Hest

I Dynasty tombs

I Dynasty tombs

I Dynasty tombs

Mastaba of Ti

Serapeum
Greek statues

Mastaba of Mereruka

Pyramid of Teti

Refreshment tent

Mastaba of Akhti-Hotep and Ptah-Hotep

Zoser's funerary complex

Pyramid of Userkaf

Causeway of Unas

Pyramid of Unas

Boat pits and mastabas

Tomb of Horemheb

Monastery of St. Jeremias

To Cairo and Memphis

Unfinished pyramid of Sekhemkhet

129

and rubble, its casing alone in hewn limestone. Nevertheless, the pyramid has proved of immense historical importance, for when Gaston Maspero entered the tomb chamber in 1881 he found the walls covered with inscriptions, the *Pyramid Texts,* which are the earliest mortuary literature of Egypt. These are hymns and rituals that preceded and accompanied the interment of the body; prayers for the release of the *ba* or soul; another section listing offerings of food, drink and clothing for use in the afterlife. Until this time, pyramids had gone unadorned. Thereafter, funerary literature underwent considerable elaboration and embroidery, culminating in that collection — or rather genre, for no such definitive compilation existed — of New Kingdom literature known to us as the Book of the Dead.

The Pyramid
Texts

Despite its exterior, the pyramid remains internally sound and you can creep down the 1.4-metre high corridor, entered from the north face, past three enormous slabs of granite meant to block the way. Unlike the New Kingdom texts which were full of advice on how to steer a course clear of the forces of evil, which in effect emphasised the dangers that preceded safe arrival in the afterlife and were the tools of the trade of a blackmailing priesthood, the Pyramid Texts celebrate eternal life and identify the deceased pharaoh with Osiris. Nevertheless, there is anxiety in the prayers. The confident era of the sun cult was waning; a personal god and a note of redemption marked the rising cult of Osiris. The state was weakening; the troubled times of the First Intermediate Period were approaching.

Visiting the Outstanding Mastabas

You can now trudge across the sands or drive to the refreshment tent which stands near the site of Mariette's house, where he stayed during those first serious explorations of Saqqara. The beer is cold and in the heat goes straight to your head. You can walk around the rest of the necropolis in a state of intoxication. When visiting the Serapeum, you may be grateful for that.

Refreshments
and Mariette's
house

But first you can visit some mastabas. The **Mastaba of Mereruka**, with 32 rooms, is the largest at Saqqara. He enjoyed in death not only elbow room, but the prestigious company to which he had become accustomed in life. For Mereruka was vizier to the Pharaoh Teti (VI Dyn), whose pyramid is next door, and he married and was buried with the boss's daughter. The *entry passage* shows Mereruka painting a picture of the seasons and playing a board game to pass away the time, while the *first three chambers* are decorated with scenes of hunting, furniture making and goldsmiths at work. At the far end of the mastaba is a *chapel* with six pillars, containing a statue of the vizier himself. The scenes to the left of this are interesting: they show the domestication of gazelles, goats and hyenas.

The double **Mastaba of Akhti-Hotep and Ptah-Hotep** is to the southeast of the refreshment tent, along your way if you are walking between the complexes of Zoser or Unas or Mereruka's mastaba and a beer. Ptah-Hotep describes himself as a priest of Maat and he may have held other positions too. At any rate, he seems to have been a very important official during the reign of Djedkare (V Dyn), predecessor of Unas. His son Akhti-Hotep was vizier, judge and chief of the granary and treasury. Their mastaba is smaller than that of Ti's, which we come to next, but is more developed and is particularly interesting for the reliefs which are in various stages of completion.

Reliefs in progress

You enter from the north and come into a *corridor*. On its left wall are preliminary drawings in red with corrections by the master artist in black. On the right wall are various stages of low relief. The background is cut away first to yield a silhouette and then the details are pencilled in and cut. In the lower registers, servants carry fowl in the arms towards Ptah-Hotep who stands at the far end of this right-hand wall. Though somewhat stylised, with his shoulders squared but with head and limbs in profile, the detailed musculature shows the artist's sound sense of anatomy.

At the top end of the corridor you turn right into a *pillared hall* and then left, passing through a *vestibule,* into *Ptah-Hotep's tomb chamber.* The ceiling imitates the trunks of palm trees while the mural reliefs, still retaining some colour, are the finest preserved of the Old Kingdom, surpassing even those in the more famous Mastaba of Ti.

Ptah-Hotep's tomb chamber; the finest Old Kingdom reliefs

On the *right wall* are two door-shaped stelae, representing the entrance to the tomb. Between them is Ptah-Hotep, depicted in the panther-skin of a high priest, seated at a cornucopian table of offerings, a goblet raised to his lips. In the upper register, priests make offerings; in the lower three rows, servants bear gifts. They are lucky to get off so lightly; during the I Dynasty they were sacrificed and interred around their master's mastaba. On the *far wall* Ptah-Hotep is again at table, this time with a stylised loaf of bread before him and copper basins and ewers alongside so that he may cleanse himself before eating. In the upper register women representing various estates bring him the products of his farms, while in the second register animals are being thrown and slaughtered. The reliefs on the *left wall* are the finest and most interesting, a catalogue of events in the life of the deceased. On the right, according to the text, Ptah-Hotep is inspecting the 'gifts and tribute that are brought by the estates of the North and South'; boys are wrestling and running, caged animals (lions, gazelles, hares and hedgehogs) are drawn up, and a cow is giving birth, a peasant guiding the calf into the world. The bottom register shows domestic poultry and the text claims that Ptah-Hotep possessed '121,000 geese of one variety, 11,210 of another variety, 120,000 small geese, 111,200 goslings and 1225 swans'. On the left of this wall Ptah-Hotep 'witnesses all the pleasant activities that take place in the whole country'. In the top registers, boys and girls are playing; there is one episode of two boys seated and facing each other as their friends vault over them. This game, called *Khaki la wizza*, is still played today by Nubians. The third register is devoted to aspects of viticulture; the fourth shows animal life (note the hare emerging from its hole with a cricket in its mouth); the fifth is a hunting scene, the cow tied as bait for the lion; the fifth and sixth registers show marsh and boating scenes.

Above the entrance is a faded mural, but you can make out Ptah-Hotep preparing for his day, a manicurist at his hands, a pedicurist at his feet, musicians entertaining him, greyhounds beneath his chair and a pet monkey held by his valet. The sophistication of this scene is all the more striking when you recall that it depicts daily Egyptian life, albeit at the very top of the social ladder, nearly 4500 years ago, that is when Europe and most of Asia were still in the Stone Age.

The purpose of tomb reliefs The purpose of these reliefs was to provide food, indeed a complete experience of life, for the ka. They began during the IV Dynasty as it was realised that relatives and descendants did not always provide fresh offerings; the reliefs were imitative magic against default. But one can also imagine the great pleasure they must have given the tomb owner, an assurance that he was going to take it all with him, and to his relatives when they did gather in his tomb. I think of some of the more elaborate marble tombs in Greek cemeteries today; they are like small shrines with an inner chamber for the deceased and an outer chamber with seats for the living, and they are the cheeriest places, often attracting bountiful picnics. Unas, a generation later, was already worried about his relationship with Osiris; but here there is not a single god, no judgement, no doubt—afterlife follows on from life as assuredly as day follows day, and without even an intervening night.

Now returning to the pillared hall you turn left for the *chamber of Akhti-Hotep,* similarly though less finely decorated. A passageway leads out of the side of this and opening off it, on your left, is a chamber containing an *anonymous mummy.* The passageway leads back to the pillared hall and the entrance corridor; while negotiating it I tripped over a skeleton, perhaps belonging to a 20th C AD tourist who had got locked in.

I have already mentioned that my brother got himself locked into the Great Pyramid; at Saqqara a friend got himself locked into the Serapeum for half an hour with the lights off (an experience that would have turned me instantly into a skeleton); and I got locked into the Mastaba of Ti, and would have spent the night there but for a ladder left providentially in the open court. If you lack Ptah-Hotep's confidence in the coming day, make certain the keeper knows you are there and looks like the sort of fellow who would let you out.

The **Mastaba of Ti** is to the north of the refreshment tent and you can follow the road that leads to the Serapeum part of the way there. The mastaba was discovered by Mariette in 1865 and has been well restored by the Egyptian Department of Antiquities. It originally stood above ground but is now entirely sunk in the sand. Its reliefs rival those in Ptah-Hotep's tomb chamber and exceed them in variety. Ti was a parvenu and royal hairdresser during the early V Dynasty; he was also overseer of several royal mortuary temples and pyramids and controller of royal ponds, farms and stock from which he evidently enriched himself. His wife was related to the royal family and his children bore the title 'royal descendant', to which Ti himself was not entitled. Ti's wife and eldest son were also entombed here, but some later would-be arriviste made off with the goods and disposed of the bodies.

In plan, the entrance is from the north, a two-pillared vestibule leading to a spacious open pillared court at the centre of which a flight of stairs descends to a subterranean passage ending in an antechamber and the tomb chamber. Otherwise, a corridor leads out from the rear of the open court and passes a chamber on the right, arriving at the funerary chamber and the serdab.

Once through the open court, whose reliefs have been badly damaged by exposure, the walls of corridors and rooms are finely decorated with familiar scenes. The most interesting room, with the most beautiful reliefs, is Ti's *funerary chamber*. Through the slot in the far (south) wall you can see Ti (this is a cast of the original statue now in the Cairo Museum) staring vacantly northwards from his serdab, lacking, I am afraid, Zoser's look of adventure. Needless to say his hair, or rather his wig, is well done. Most enjoyable are the *reliefs on the near (north) wall,* all concerned with life in the marshes of the Delta. Look particularly at the central relief of Ti *sailing through the marshes.*

**Hippopotamus
hunt**

This is a classic representation of a hippopotamus hunt; the hippopotamus, to the lower right, has seized a crocodile which, meanwhile, is desperately trying to bite the hippo's leg. Ti is shown larger than his huntsmen who, from another boat, are harpooning the hippo. Below the boats are fine Nile fish of different species, identifiable as favoured catches in the river today. On the right, in a small boat with a curiously truncated stern, a fisherman is about to club a large schal fish over the head. Above Ti, amongst the papyrus clusters, birds are being attacked in their nests by carnivorous animals, the reeds bending with their weight. In the register below is a line of *elegant female bearers,* their transparent coloured dresses surrendered to time, their nakedness and varied poses freshly pleasing.

This relief is unusual for having two layers of meaning. Literally it is a hunt in the marshes; but symbolically it is Ti against the forces of evil and chaos. The hippopotamus was particularly feared and hated in ancient Egypt, but Ti together with a helpful crocodile is killing it. Fish and birds represented chaos, but here again man and animals are subduing them.

By way of making amends for having locked me in Ti's tomb, the keeper afterwards invited me to his little concrete hut for a glass of mint tea. It was clearly his eagerness to retreat here, out of the blistering heat, that caused my incarceration in the first place. We sat on a reed mat on the floor while he manipulated various soda cans over his burner—some of the cans for storing the water, one for boiling it, others for decanting the tea—and we smoked his hubbly-bubbly meanwhile. This he lit with bits of dried corncob he kept for the purpose and brought to a glow in the burner flame. The surrounding necropolis, my temporary entombment, the sand and heat were all forgotten in this humble private place where tea and tobacco were prepared and consumed with meticulous ritual. The keeper fussed and bubbled and tasted and grunted with the fullness of it all, and as we drank the thick sweet tea, so satisfying, and enjoyed the relaxation of the waterpipe, we looked out as from a serdab upon the desert wasteland and he called this tea and this tobacco his friends.

Tombs of the Apis Bulls

The Serapeum is the strangest place at Saqqara. A temple once stood here amidst the sands but what remain are the long underground galleries cut through the rock where the Apis bulls were buried. This was Mariette's great discovery in 1851 which began the serious excavation of Saqqara that has continued ever since. Entry is to the west of the refreshment tent; you follow the road which first bends right towards Ti's mastaba and then turns left. At this second bend was Mariette's house, and immediately by the roadside, on your left and under the protective roof, is the surprising sight of several Greek statues arranged in a semicircle. These and their unlikely connection with bull burial requires some explanation.

Tea in the desert

The strangest place at Saqqara

The huge tombs of these Apis bulls were previously known only from references to them by various writers of antiquity. For instance, Herodotus wrote: 'The Apis is the calf of a cow which is never afterwards able to have another. The Egyptian belief is that a flash of light descends upon the cow from heaven, and this causes her to receive Apis. The Apis-calf has distinctive marks; it is black, with a white diamond on its forehead, the image of an eagle on its back, the hairs on its tail double, and a scarab under its tongue'. Apis thus miraculously conceived was considered to be an incarnation of Ptah, the god of Memphis. Worshipped as such during his lifetime within a special sanctuary in the Temple of Ptah, he was mummified after his death on those alabaster beds you can still see amongst the few surviving stones of Memphis. Then, identified with Osiris under the name Osiris-Apis, he was taken with great pomp to these underground galleries at the Serapeum and placed within a gigantic sarcophagus.

Sacred bull cults go back into the prehistory of Egypt, and during the I and II Dynasties a bull would wander across the field of the Heb-Sed race, symbolically fertilising the two lands. But animal cults enjoyed an astonishing popularity during the Late Egyptian Period as the old beliefs degenerated. Herodotus, attempting to demonstrate the madness of Cambyses, the Persian ruler of Egypt, records that 'the priests brought Apis and Cambyses, half mad as he was, drew his dagger, aimed a blow at its belly, but missed and struck its thigh. Then he laughed, and said to the priests: "Do you call that a god, you poor creatures? Are your gods flesh and blood? Do they feel the prick of steel? No doubt a god like that is good enough for the Egyptians; but you won't get away with trying to make a fool of me"'', and he had the priests whipped and forbade the cult, but when finally Apis died of his wounds he was buried by the priests without the knowledge of Cambyses. In this instance, at least, Cambyses sounds quite sane, but it is understandable that the once mighty priesthood should cling to some tangible shred of belief as the old order was being attacked by foreign rulers. The Ptolemies were more shrewd and flattered the priesthood, encouraged their cults, built temples and ruled Egypt for 300 years.

The galleries of the Serapeum date from three periods, the earliest to the reign of Ramses II (XIX Dyn), enlarged by his son Khaemwas; a second to the reign of Psammetichus I (XXVI Dyn); and a main gallery to the Ptolemies. It was the Greek Ptolemies who encouraged an identity between Osiris and Dionysos, and Plutarch comments that 'as for what the priests openly do in the burial of the Apis when they transport its carcass on a raft, this in no way falls short

135

of Bacchic revelry, for they wear fawn-skins and carry thyrsus-rods' — a staff tipped with a pine cone, in short a phallus — 'and produce shouts and movements as do the ecstatic celebrants of the Dionysiac orgies'. (Recall the sarcophagus of the dwarf in Room 49 on the ground floor of the Cairo Museum.) It is from the Ptolemaic period that the **semicircle of Greek statues** of poets and philosophers dates. Homer is at the centre, Pindar plays the lyre at the far right, and at the far left is a base inscribed with the name of Plato. They must be turning over in their graves.

Mariette was led to the Serapeum by recalling a quotation from Strabo (24 BC): 'One finds at Memphis a temple to Serapis in such a sandy place that the wind heaps up sand dunes beneath which we saw sphinxes, some half-buried, some buried up to the head, from which one can suppose that the way to the temple could not be without danger if one were caught in a sudden wind-storm'. Mariette had found one such head at Saqqara, and removing the sand in the area found an entire avenue of sphinxes leading to the Greek statues and to the Serapeum galleries. The avenue has since sanded up again.

Mariette's description of his discovery of the Serapeum

Saqqara can seem strange enough today. When Mariette was excavating here, he described the conditions in his house: 'Snakes slithered along the floor, tarantulas or scorpions swarmed in the wall crevices, large spider webs waved from the ceiling like flags. As soon as night fell, bats, attracted by the light, entered my cell through the cracks in the door and kept me awake with their spectral flights. Before going to sleep, I tucked the edges of my mosquito net beneath my mattress and put my trust in God and all the saints, while outside jackals, hyenas and wolves howled around the house'. Of entering the Serapeum, Mariette wrote: 'When I first penetrated into the sepulchre of the Apis, I was so overcome with astonishment that, though it is now five years ago, the feeling is still vivid in my mind. By some inexplicable accident one chamber of the Apis tombs, walled up in the thirtieth year of Ramses II, had escaped the general plunder of the monuments, and I was so fortunate as to find it untouched. Three thousand seven hundred years had had no effect in altering its primitive state. The finger mark of the Egyptian who set the last stone in the wall built up to cover the door was still visible in the mortar. Bare feet had left their traces on the sand strewn in a corner of this chamber of the dead; nothing had been disturbed in this burying-place where an embalmed ox had been resting for nearly forty centuries'.

A terrifying moronic force

My own recollection was of Robin Fedden's words: 'One has the impression of a terrifying moronic force at work, for the tombs reveal the endemic stupidity of man'. You descend a ramp slipping under the formless desert surface and reach a *corridor* leading off to left and right. Down to the left it meets a *transverse gallery* and left into that, on the left, within a vault, is a massive *pink granite sarcophagus* with panels and across the top edge hieroglyphs—on the right an Apis bull is depicted with the characteristic black markings. The rest of this gallery is blocked off by a grate.

You now reverse direction, heading down a 150-metre gallery. On either side, in alternating succession, are more vaults, in all but one of which squats a monstrous black sarcophagus—bull-size. The *finest sarcophagus* of all is at the very end of this gallery, on the right, with carved decoration and polished to a glassy lustre. You can climb down into its pit and stand on a step at the back to peer inside.

Until a few years ago the Serapeum was lit only at lengthy intervals by dim yellow lights which in the murky darkness case a greenish-glow. At some places, the lights would have gone out and you had to walk through velvety blackness. In the silence and the dim light, the repetition of vaults and sarcophagi became like a bad dream you could not awake from, and you just walked on, with literally no light at the end of the tunnel. It was macabre, and with your capillaries shot full with beer you achieved enough perspective to find it utterly incredible that the Ptolemies, whose gallery this is, could have perpetuated anything so repulsive and outlandish. The lighting has now been greatly 'improved'—and perhaps also I have recovered from my first shock; but what was once the weirdest place in Egypt seems now to be only as blandly repulsive as, say, walking down a corridor of Cairo's Marriott Hotel.

It was not here, but in the Rammesid gallery, now inaccessible, that Mariette found the one untouched Apis tomb, a mummified bull inside, and also in the gallery the mummy of Khaemwas, who had been appointed by his father Ramses II High Priest of Ptah. And there he found those ancient footprints. You notice footprints in the sand in this Ptolemaic gallery too, of more recent visitors, and they bring to mind, as so often encounters with Egypt's pharaonic past do, our own voyages into the cosomos, those footprints left in the dust on the surface of the windless Moon which may remain for millions of years undisturbed.

Retracing your steps from the end of the main gallery, turn to the left and then to the right. An *empty sarcophagus* almost blocks the route. A little farther on is its lid. It seems to have been abandoned before the interment of the sacred bull, suggesting the cult was abruptly ended.

Other Animal Cults at Saqqara

This account of Saqqara has covered only the most major **The search for** points of interest to the layman. There is a search now **Imhotep's tomb** going on for Imhotep's tomb which is thought to be to the northeast of the Serapeum and the Mastaba of Ti. In this area have been found the Anubieion, sacred to Anubis, with a gallery for dogs; the galleries of the Bubasteion, sacred to Bastet, filled with mummified cats; the Temple of Thoth, its galleries piled with thousands of mummified ibises, baboons and falcons; and the Isieion, the Temple of Isis, with underground galleries containing the sarcophagi of the sacred cows that had given birth to the Apis bulls. It is possible that these stacks of smaller mummified creatures were brought over hundreds of years by pilgrims as offerings to a favoured god, or as supplication by those seeking a cure. It is because of these associations with healing cults that Imhotep's shrine and tomb might be here; he was later worshipped as the god of medicine, the Egyptian equivalent of Asclepios. These cults continued into the Roman period and were only finally suppressed several centuries into our era by the victory of Christianity over paganism, when the fashion changed from dogs, cats, birds and baboons to collecting bits of martyrs' bodies.

Pyramids Farther South

The **necropolis of Dahshur** is a few kilometres to the south of Saqqara. Of its four pyramids, two date from the Middle Kingdom and are badly ruined—they are likely to be of interest only to the specialist. Snofru's **Bent and Red Pyramids**, already referred to in an earlier chapter, are the chief attraction. But this is a military area, and foreign tourists are not permitted entry. Instead you should stand on the southern ramparts of Zoser's funerary complex to see these great pyramids resting upon an endless plain confronting only the cosmos.

Much farther south is the **Meidum pyramid**, or what remains of it. This was the first attempt at a true pyramid (see *The Pyramid Age* chapter) and the lessons learnt from its monumental failure, if one accepts Mendelssohn's theory, led to the successful completion of those greatest pyramids of all at Giza. For that reason, but also for the spectacle of this abrupt tower on the desert's edge, the Meidum pyramid is as much worth visiting as any.

PRACTICAL INFORMATION

You can reach **Saqqara** by horse or camel from the Giza Pyramids (see previous chapter), though you will not be left with much time to explore the site, and a visit to Memphis would probably be out of the question. (You can, however, hire a camel *at* Saqqara for a little trot round the site.) There is also a bus to Bradrashein, a village near Memphis; ask about it at the Mena House or the Tourist Police at the Pyramids. And there are tours or a taxi from Cairo. Refreshments and light meals are available at the Saqqara site. There is no **site fee for Memphis**. The **site fee for Saqqara** is LE5, or LE2 for students.

Dahshur is in the midst of a military area and is off-limits to foreign tourists. Specialists may be able to obtain permission from the Ministry of the Interior, Midan Lazouli, Cairo.

Tours do not include Meidum with Memphis and Saqqara. But ask, eg at Thomas Cook, if it can be included at an extra cost. If driving to **Meidum**, follow the road along the west bank of the Nile south towards El Wasta; the pyramid will appear on your right but you drive past it a bit until you come to a paved road signposted for the pyramid in English and Arabic. This heads off into the desert, at first passing south of the pyramid and then coming up to its northwest corner.

APPENDIX

Money
100 piastres (PT) = 1 Egyptian pound (LE). At the moment of publication, $1 = LE2.50, and £1 = LE4.00

Arabic Numerals
It is important that you learn to recognise Arabic numerals (read from left to right, like ours) — this will prove a great help when shopping or catching numbered buses.

ARABIC NUMERALS

Chronology
The chapter *Cairo: Mother of the World* includes a useful summary of the city's history. Below, in simple date form, important events of the Islamic period are included in a chronology extending from pharaonic times to the present.

Pharaonic Dynasties
Early Dynastic Period (3100–2700 BC)
First Dynasty
Menes (Narmer) — unification of Egypt; capital at Memphis.
Second Dynasty
Old Kingdom (2700–2200 BC) — period of stability.
Third Dynasty (2700–2650 BC)
Zoser (2700 BC) — start of the Pyramid Age.
Fourth Dynasty (2650–2500 BC)
Snofru (2650 BC)
Cheops (2600 BC)
Chephren (2560 BC)
Mycerinus (2525 BC) — end of the Pyramid Age.
Fifth Dynasty (2500–2350 BC)
Unas (2375 BC) — Pyramid Texts.
Sixth Dynasty (2350–2200 BC) — period of decline.
First Intermediate Period (2200–2050 BC) — collapse of central authority.
Seventh and Eighth Dynasties (2180–2155)
Ninth and Tenth Dynasties (2155–2055 BC)

Eleventh Dynasty (2135–2000 BC)
Mentuhotep II (2060–2010 BC) — reunites Egypt; capital at Thebes.
Middle Kingdom (2050–1800 BC)
Twelfth Dynasty (1990–1780 BC) — royal residence returns to Memphis.
Second Intermediate Period (1800–1550 BC) — collapse of central authority.
Thirteenth through Seventeenth Dynasties (1780–1570 BC)
Hyksos rule in Lower Egypt (1730–1570 BC) — introduction of the chariot.
New Kingdom (1570–1090 BC) — period of power, luxury and cosmopolitanism.
Eighteenth Dynasty (1570–1305 BC) — period of greatest contribution to the splendour of Thebes and Karnak.
Ahmosis I (1570–1545 BC) — expels Hyksos; establishes royal residence, and religious and political capital at Thebes.
Tuthmosis I (1525–1495 BC) — burials begin at Valley of the Kings.
Tuthmosis III (1490–1436 BC) — struggle with Hatshepsut; after her passing, he lays foundation of Asian and African empire.
Hatshepsut (1486–1468 BC)
Amenophis III (1398–1361 BC) — apogee of New Kingdom opulence.
Amenophis IV (Akhenaton) (1369–1353 BC) — assault on priesthood of Amun; establishes worship of the Aton.
Smenkhkere (1355–1352 BC)
Tutankhaton (Tutankhamun) (1352–1344 BC) — return to orthodoxy; after his death, rule by military dictatorship.
Nineteenth Dynasty (1303–1200 BC) — restoration of royal power.
Ramses I (1303–1302 BC)
Seti I (1302–1290 BC) — new building work in Old Kingdom style.
Ramses II (1290–1224 BC) — prodigious builder, eg Ramesseum and Abu Simbel.
Merneptah (1224–1214 BC) — possibly the pharaoh of the Exodus.
Syrian interregnum (1202–1197 BC)
Twentieth Dynasty (1200–1090 BC) — dislocations as Egypt enters Iron Age.
Ramses III (1195–1164 BC) — defeats Sea

Peoples; succeeded by incompetent rulers.

Late Dynastic Period (1090–332 BC)—period of decline; often foreign rule.

Twenty-first Dynasty (1090–945 BC)

Twenty-second Dynasty (945–745 BC)—warriors of Libyan origin.

Sheshonk I (945 BC)—loots Jerusalem (I Kings 14,25–26)

Twenty-third Dynasty (745–718 BC)—Ethiopian kings control Upper Egypt.

Twenty-fourth Dynasty (718–712 BC)—Ethiopian kings control all Egypt.

Twenty-fifth Dynasty (712–663 BC)

Taharka (659–671 BC)—Ethiopian king defeated by Assyrians who sack Thebes.

Twenty-sixth Dynasty (663–525 BC)—Delta rulers, their capital at Sais; Assyrians ejected with Greek help.

Twenty-seventh Dynasty (525–404 BC)

Cambyses (525–522 BC)

Darius I (522–486 BC)

Xerxes the Great (486–466 BC)—Persian rule.

Twenty-eighth Dynasty (404–399 BC)—Persians ejected with Greek help.

Twenty-ninth Dynasty (399–380 BC)—Delta remains the vital centre of power.

Thirtieth Dynasty (380–343 BC)

Nectanebos I (380–343 BC)—great builder, eg at Philae.

Thirty-first Dynasty (343–332 BC)—Persian rule.

Alexander enters Egypt in 332 BC

The Ptolemies

After the death of Alexander (323 BC), his empire was divided between three of his Macedonian generals, Ptolemy taking Egypt. He established a dynasty which ruled the country for 300 years in the guise of pharaohs, albeit Greek-speaking ones. The last of the dynasty was Cleopatra VII.

51–30 BC: Cleopatra VII. Ruled jointly with her younger brother Ptolemy III who banished her (48 BC), but in the same year she received the support of Julius Caesar and Ptolemy was drowned in the Nile. Bore Caesar a son (47 BC). Caesar assassinated (44 BC). Met Antony (41 BC). The battle of Actium (31 BC). Suicide of Antony and Cleopatra;

Octavian (Augustus) makes Egypt a province of the Roman Empire (30 BC).

Roman and Byzantine Periods

30 BC: *Octavian* (Augustus) incorporates Egypt into the Roman Empire.

c. AD 30: Crucifixion of *Jesus* at Jerusalem.

AD 45: *St Mark* makes his first convert to Christianity in Egypt, a Jewish shoemaker of Alexandria.

AD 284–305: Reign of *Diocletian*. His accession marks the beginning of the 'Era of Martyrs' from which the Copts date their calendar. Persecution of the Christians (AD 303).

AD 324–37: Reign of *Constantine the Great*. Converts to Christianity. Founds Constantinople (AD 330).

AD 379–95: Reign of *Theodosius I*. Declares Christianity to be the religion of the Roman Empire.

AD 395: Partition of the Roman Empire into East (Constantinople) and West (Rome). Notional date for the beginning of the Byzantine Empire.

AD 451: Council of Chalcedon declares monophysitism a heresy, effectively expelling the Egyptian (Coptic) Church from the main body of Christianity.

AD 476: Fall of the Roman Empire in the West.

AD 622: *Mohammed's* flight from Mecca, the *hegira*, from which the Muslim calendar is reckoned. His death (AD 632).

AD 640: An Arab force under *Amr* enters Egypt. Fortress of Babylon taken (AD 641). Fustat founded.

Arab and Turkish Periods

All dates are according to the Western calendar (AD).

661: Murder of *Ali*, son-in-law of the Prophet; the caliphate passes to the Umayyads.

661–750: The *Umayyad Caliphate*, with its capital at Damascus, rules over a united Arab empire stretching from the borders of China to the shores of the Atlantic, and up into France.

750–935: *Abbassids and Tulunids*. The Abbassids put a bloody end to the Umayyads in Syria and succeed to caliphate, ruling the Arab world from Baghdad. *Ibn Tulun*, an Abbassid

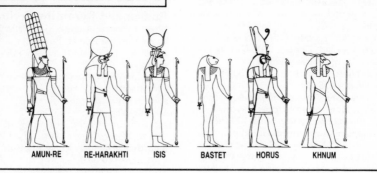

GODS OF ANCIENT EGYPT

AMUN-RE RE-HARAKHTI ISIS BASTET HORUS KHNUM

governor of Egypt, makes himself independent of Baghdad and establishes a dynasty (**870–935**).

c.820: The Copts, resentful of their Arab conquerors, rise in revolt several times during the 8th and 9th C. After their defeat, the majority of Copts convert to Islam.

969–1171: The *Fatimid Caliphate* in Egypt, which now follows Shi'a rather than Sunni Islam. Cairo, its capital, founded (**969**). Al-Azhar founded (**971**). The Fatimid empire reaches its peak under *Caliph Abu Mansur al-Aziz* (**975–96**). He introduces the practice of importing slave troops, the forerunners of the Mamelukes. His successor, *al-Hakim* (**996–1021**), is an all-powerful psychotic; the decline of the Fatimid empire begins with his death.

1099: The Crusaders take Jerusalem.

1171–1250: The *Ayyubids;* the dynasty of *Saladin,* a Kurd from Syria. He converts Egypt back to Sunni Islam. Drives the Crusaders from Jerusalem (**1187**). The Mamelukes rise to power during the rule of *Shagarat al-Durr* (**1249–57**).

1250–1382: The *Bahri Mamelukes.* The most celebrated of these Mameluke sultans are *Baybars* (**1260–77**); *Qalaun* (**1279–90**); *al-Nasr* (**1309–40**) — the beautiful mausolea of these last two are on Sharia Muizz in Cairo; and *al-Hassan* (**1347–51, 1354–61**), builder of the great madrasa bearing his name.

1382–1517: The *Burgi Mamelukes.* The most celebrated of these Mameluke sultans are *Barquq* (**1382–89, 1390–98**), whose mosque is on Sharia Muizz; his mausoleum in the City of the Dead in Cairo; *Baybars* (**1422–38**), whose mausoleum is in the City of the Dead; *Qaytbay* (**1468–95**), known for his fortress on the site of the Pharos in Alexandria, and his mausoleum in the City of the Dead; and *al-Ghuri* (**1500–16**) whose monuments stand near Al-Azhar. *Tumanbay* (**1516–17**) was the last of the Burgi sultans; he was hanged three times by the Turks outside Bab Zuwayla in Cairo.

1517: The Rule of the *Ottoman Turks* begins in Egypt and continues, if only nominally, until 1914.

The Modern Period

1798–1801: *French occupation* of Egypt. *Napoleon* lands at Alexandria; Battle of the Pyramids; Battle of the Nile (**1798**). *Napoleon* departs from Egypt (**1799**). A British Army compels the French to evacuate the country (**1801**)

1805: *Mohammed Ali* becomes Viceroy of Egypt and after massacring the Mamelukes (**1811**) becomes, effectively, the independent ruler of Egypt, establishing a dynasty that was to end with *Farouk.*

1869: Opening of the Suez Canal during the reign of *Ismail.*

1882: Nationalist uprising led by *Arabi. British occupation* of Egypt begins.

1936: Anglo-Egyptian Treaty, formally ending British occupation. British army withdraws, except from the Canal Zone.

1939–45: Egypt nominally neutral during the Second World War, but British Army invited to return to fight the encroaching Germans.

1952: 23 July, *Nasser's* group stages a coup. 26 July, *King Farouk* abdicates and leaves the country.

1953: Egypt declared a *republic*.

1954: *Nasser* becomes head of state.

1954–56: British evacuate the Canal Zone.

1956: Israel invades Sinai in collusion with a British and French troop landing in the Canal Zone. Britain, France and Israel withdraw after international protest.

1967: The June 'Six Day War'. Israel attacks and defeats Egypt, occupies all of Sinai. The Suez Canal is blocked.

1970: *Nasser* dies. *Anwar Sadat* becomes President.

1973: October, Egyptian forces cross the Canal and drive back the Israeli army. Israeli forces continue to occupy the Gaza Strip and most of Sinai.

1975: Suez Canal reopened.

1977: *Sadat* visits Jerusalem in a dramatic peace bid.

1980: Egypt and Israel exchange ambassadors.

1981: 6 October, *Sadat* assassinated. *Hosni Mubarak* becomes president later that month.

1982: Israel evacuates Sinai.

1984: Egypt's first free elections since 1952.

GLOSSARY

Abu: The Arabic for saint, whether Muslim or Christian. Holy man.

Amun God of Thebes; he was made a sun god under the name *Amun-Re* and became the national god during the New Kingdom. His sacred animal was the ram. Along with his wife, *Mut,* and their son, *Khonsu,* Amun was one of the Theban triad.

Ankh: The hieroglyphic sign for 'life', resembling a cross with a loop in place of the upper arm.

Anubis: God of the dead, associated with interment. His sacred animal was the dog or jackal.

Apis: The sacred bull of Memphis, buried in the Serapeum at Saqqara.

Apse: A semi-circular domed recess, most frequently at the east end of a church.

Aton: The sun's disc; the life force. Worshipped by Akhenaton, who attacked the priesthood of Amun.

Atum: The creator god of Heliopolis, represented as a man.

Azan: The Muslim call to prayer (see *muezzin*).

Ba: A spirit that inhabits the body during life but is not attached to it; at death it leaves the body and joins the divine spirit. (See *ka*.)

Bab: A gate, as Bab Zuwayla.

Basilica: A church in the form of a long colonnaded hall, usually with one or more apses at the east end, and a narthex at the west end.

Bastet: The goddess of Bubastis, a goddess of joy. Her sacred animal was the lioness or cat.

Bayt: A house, or the self-contained apartments into which Omayyad mansions and Abbasid palaces were divided.

Canopic jars: Containers placed within ancient tombs to preserve those organs and viscera thought essential for the dead man's continued existence in the afterlife.

Capitals: Pharaonic and Ptolemaic temples employed capitals decorated either with plant forms (*palmiform, papyriform, lotiform*) or other motifs (*Hathoric,* ie with the human face and cow's ears of Hathor; forms deriving from timber construction eg *tent poles*).

Cartouche: In hieroglyphics, the oval band enclosing the god's or pharaoh's name and symbolising unchanging continuity.

Cavetto cornice: One of the most characteristic decorative features in ancient Egyptian architecture, a concave moulding decorated with palmettes. It was used along the tops of walls and *pylons,* projecting at front and sides. Below it would be a narrow convex *torus* moulding.

Colours: Primary colours usually had particular applications and significance in ancient Egyptian painting. *Black* represented death: mummies, also Osiris as king of the dead, were commonly depicted in black. *Blue* was for sky and water, the sky gods painted this colour. *Green* was the colour of rebirth: Osiris, who overcame death and was reborn, often had his face and limbs painted green; also the solar disc was commonly painted light green on sarcophagi, instead of its usual red. *Red* was for blood and fire; men's bodies were depicted as reddish brown or brown; it also had a maleficent connotation: Seth was painted reddish brown. *White* represented silver and was the colour of the moon; it was also the colour of the garments of the gods and the crown of Upper Egypt. *Yellow* represented gold and was also used as the colour for women's bodies until the mid-XVIII Dynasty; thereafter the only women painted this colour were goddesses.

Columns: Like capitals, ancient columns followed certain decorative motifs, eg papyrus columns modelled after either a single stem and therefore smooth, or after a bundle of stems and therefore ribbed.

Crowns: The red crown of Lower Egypt was joined with the white crown of Upper Egypt to represent unification of the country (see *colours*). The blue crown or headdress was worn when riding a chariot; it appears after the introduction of the horse into Egypt by the Hyksos c. 1600 BC. No matter what headdress the pharaoh wore, he was always shown with the *uraeus* on his forehead.

Electrum: An alloy of gold and silver. The tips of obelisks were covered with electrum. In ancient Egypt, where gold was mined in abundance, both silver and electrum were more precious than gold alone.

Evil eye: The superstition that the envious glance of any passer-by, attracted by an immodest show of wealth, achievement or beauty, can harm or bewitch. Reciting certain verses of the Koran is one way of warding it off. *Uzait Horun*, the Eye of Horus, is meant to ensure safety and happiness and wards off the evil eye; it may be painted on cars, trucks and fishing boats, or worn as an amulet, particularly by children, who are especially vulnerable. Children also leave their handprints on walls to avert the evil eye. The probable value of the belief is as a social control, minimising at least the appearance of disparity in people's fortunes and so promoting solidarity.

Exonarthex: The outer vestibule of a church.

Fellahin: Egyptian peasants. The singular is *fellah*.

Flagellum: A flail or rattle to drive away evil spirits; it could be used only by a pharaoh and so represented the royal authority in carvings and statues. In the other hand was the *crook*, another royal symbol.

Hajj: The pilgrimage to Mecca that all Muslims should make at least once in their lifetime. When they have done so, they will often paint a scene of the event on their houses.

Hamam: A bath, public or private.

Harem: The private family (or specifically the women's) quarter in a house.

Hathor: The goddess of heaven, joy and love; the Greeks identified her with *Aphrodite*. She was the deity of Dendera and protector of the Theban necropolis. Her sacred animal was the cow.

Heb-Sed: The jubilee marking the thirtieth year of a pharaoh's reign (see Saqqara).

Hegira: Mohammed's flight, or more properly his 'withdrawal of affection', from Mecca in AD 622. The Muslim calendar starts from this date.

Herakhte: A form of *Horus*. 'Horus of the horizon', often combined with the sun god as *Re-Herakhte* and so worshipped at Heliopolis. The falcon was sacred to him.

Horus: The son of *Isis* and *Osiris*, and revered as the sun god. He was represented as the sun disc or a falcon, his sacred animal.

Hypostyle: a hypostyle hall is any chamber whose ceiling is supported by columns or pillars.

Iconostasis: The screen carrying icons between the main part of a church and the sanctuary or choir.

Isis: Sister and wife to *Osiris*, mother of *Horus*, the patron goddess of Philae. She was highly revered at a late period. Her sacred animal was the vulture.

Ithyphallic: Denoting the erect phallus of a depicted god or pharaoh, most commonly the god *Min*. It was a sign of fertility.

Ka: A spirit that inhabits the body during life and may leave it in death, but requires the continued existence of the body (hence mummification or, by substitution, ka statues) for its survival. The ka was personal and individual, in a sense the ideal image of a man's own life. (See *ba*.)

Khan: See *wakala*.

Khnum: The patron god of Elephantine Island and the Cataracts. He fashioned man on his potter's wheel. His sacred animal was the ram.

Khonsu: Son of *Amun* and *Mut*; god of the moon. The falcon was sacred to him.

Kufic: An early style of Arabic calligraphy with angular letters.

Lily: The plant identified with Upper Egypt.

Liwan: A vaulted hall *(see mosque)*.

Maat: The goddess of truth, whose symbol was the ostrich feather. Maat is actually the deification of a concept which Egyptians strove for, both personally and for the state. As well as truth, one can attempt to define it as justice, correctness, balance. The best definition is the now rare English word meet.

Madrasa: see *mosque*.

Mashrabiyya: Interlaced wooden screenwork, used for example to cover street-facing windows in a house.

Mausoleum: A domed chamber with one or more tombs inside; though simple in form, these structures, characteristic of the City of the Dead, are of considerable beauty.

Mihrab: The niche in the *qibla wall* of a mosque, indicating the direction of Mecca.

Min: The god of the harvest, frequently amalgamated with *Amun*. He was *ithyphallically* represented. The Greeks identified him with Pan.

Minbar: The pulpit in a mosque from which the Friday prayer is spoken.

Monophysitism: The Christian doctrine that the two natures of Christ (human and divine) are absorbed into one nature (the divine). This is Coptic belief; the Latin and Greek Churches are Dyophysite, holding that Christ has two natures, unmixed and unchangeable but also indistinguishable and inseparable (Council of Chalcedon, 451).

Mont: A Theban god of war, represented by a falcon's head.

Mosque: The first mosque was the courtyard of Mohammed's house at Medina, with no architectural refinements except a shaded area at one end. Indeed, the only requirement for a mosque is that it should demarcate a space in which people may gather for saying prayers, eg an open quadrangle marked off by a ditch. From this notion developed the congregational mosque, of which the Ibn Tulun is the most outstanding example. Among noncongregational mosques are two special types which are of Cairene inspiration and development, the cruciform madrasa and the sabil kuttab. The madrasa served as a theological college, introduced by Saladin to combat Fatimid Shi'ism. Later it became more complex, a tomb appended and the madrasa formed of four *liwans*, each opening into a central court, hence cruciform. The outsanding example of this type is the Hassan. This pattern was subsequently modified, the court covered over, the east and west liwans reduced to vestigial proportions, a Koranic school for boys (*kuttab*) added as a floor above, a public fountain (*sabil*) below.

Muezzin: A crier who, as from a minaret, calls the faithful to prayer (*azan*).

Mut: The wife of *Amun* and mother of *Khonsu*. Her sacred animal was the vulture.

Naos: The enclosed inner 'house of the god' (also *cella*), the central room of a temple, though sometimes referring to the entire temple. The sanctuary.

Narthex: The entrance vestibule at the west end of a church.

Naskhi: A cursive form of Arabic writing, subsequent to *Kufic*.

Nut: Goddess of the sky, often shown supported by *Shu*.

Okel: See *wakala*.

Osiris: Originally a vegetation god, later the god of the underworld. Murdered and dismembered by *Seth*, he was the husband of *Isis* and father of *Horus*.

Papyrus: The plant identified with Lower Egypt.

Pronaos: A columned porch, leading to the *naos*.

Ptah: The patron god of Memphis and father of the gods. His sacred animal was the bull (*Apis*).

Pylon: Arranged in pairs, forming a monumental gateway to a temple. Where there are several sets of pylons, each preceeding a court, they descend in size as the sanctuary of the god is approached, while the floor level rises, creating a focussing or tunnelling effect.

Pyramidion: The capstone of a pyramid.

Qibla wall: The wall of a mosque facing Mecca.

Ramadan: The Muslim month of fasting from dawn to sunset. As the Muslim calendar is lunar, it advances against the Western solar calendar by approximately 11 days each year. Ramadan begins in 1990 on 28 March; in 1991 on 17 March; in 1992 on 5 March.

Re: The sun god, usually combined with another god, eg *Amun-Re* or *Re-Herakhte*. His priesthood was at Heliopolis.

Riwaq: The arcade around a *sahn*, or a student apartment within the arcade.

Sabil Kuttab: See *mosque*.

Sahn: An interior court, usually in a mosque.

Sakiya: An irrigation device consisting of buckets attached to a wheel which lifts water to the fields and is driven by circling oxen.

Sekhmet: The lion goddess of war.

Serapis: A god invented by the Ptolemies, looking like Zeus but identified with *Osiris-Apis*.

Seth: Brother and slayer of *Osiris*, adversary of *Horus*, he became a god of war, though after the XXII Dynasty he was reduced to the god of the impure. His sacred animal was possibly the aardvark.

Shaduf: A simple lever device for lifting water to irrigate the fields. It is operated by hand.

Shu: The god of the air. He is often shown supporting Nut.

Sobek: God of the waters, patron of the Fayyum, the crocodile was sacred to him.

Squinches: Small arches or supports across the corners of a square, enabling the carriage of a dome.

Stele: An upright stone slab or pillar with an inscription or design, used as a monument or grave marker.

Thoth: A moon deity and the god of science. The ibis and baboon were sacred to him.

Torus: A convex moulding (see *cavetto cornice*).

Uraeus: The cobra worn on the forehead of a pharaoh as both an emblem and an instrument of protection, breathing flames and destroying enemies.

Ushabti: A mummiform figurine, serving in the tomb as deputy for the dead man, carrying out his labour obligations.

Wakala: An inn for travelling merchants built around a courtyard, with stables and warehouses at ground level and living accommodation above. Other names are *khan* and *okel*.

Waqf: An endowment for the upkeep of a mosque, eg a nearby apartment house, or shops built into the street level of the mosque, earning rents.

Ziyadah: The outer court of a mosque.

ISLAMIC ARCHITECTURAL FEATURES

ARCHES

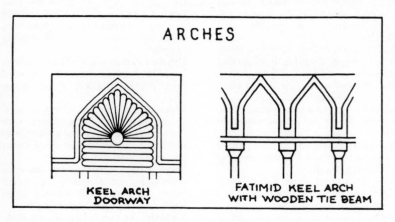

KEEL ARCH
DOORWAY

FATIMID KEEL ARCH
WITH WOODEN TIE BEAM

MINARETS

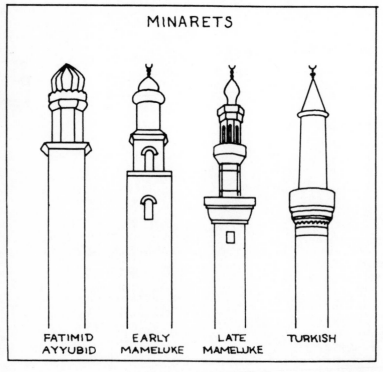

FATIMID
AYYUBID

EARLY
MAMELUKE

LATE
MAMELUKE

TURKISH

INDEX